T0194264

Praise for
Rare Bird

"Profound, tender, honest—and utterly unforgettable."
—GRETCHEN RUBIN, author of *New York Times* #1 bestseller,
The Happiness Project

"*Rare Bird* is not just another well-written story of love, loss, and the aftermath of death, but it is a story that clearly shows the constant presence and grace of a loving God. It gives assurance and comfort to those whose hearts are grieving and hope to those who are afraid."
—MARY C. NEAL, MD, *New York Times* best-selling author of
To Heaven and Back

"This is not a book; it is a kaleidoscope. With every turn of the page, a new discovery is made that forever alters your view of pain, joy, heartache, time, hope, and healing. As I journeyed through Anna's divinely written prose, I found myself unable to stand by as a passive recipient of her message. I needed to act. Because of Anna and Jack, I talked with my child about heaven. I walked around the pool's edge to sit beside a grieving woman. I looked into the darkest places of my soul and for the first time, I did not look away. If you yearn to stop hiding from that which prevents you from truly living, step into the kaleidoscope that is *Rare Bird*. Turn the page—wake up, stand up, comfort, love, and live. Turn the page—let your eyes be opened to the light that exists in whatever darkness you face."
—RACHEL MACY STAFFORD, *New York Times* best-selling
author of *Hands Free Mama*

"In her beautiful, clear-eyed prose Anna brings to life complex miracles: that the anchor of being strong is tied to feelings of unbearable weakness; that the ache of grief is often accompanied by glittering beauty; and that all we do not understand is more important to making sense of life than what we know. Her story, as well as Jack's story, is gorgeous, bold, and true, and no one will be unchanged in reading it."

    —STACY MORRISON, editor in chief and VP of Content
    Programming for BlogHer; author of *Falling Apart*
    in One Piece

rare bird

a memoir of loss and love

Anna Whiston-Donaldson

Foreword by Glennon Doyle Melton, founder of Momastery.com

CONVERGENT

BOOKS

RARE BIRD
PUBLISHED BY CONVERGENT BOOKS

All Scripture quotations and paraphrases are taken from the Holy Bible, New International Version®, NIV®. Copyright © 1973, 1978, 1984 by Biblica Inc.™ Used by permission of Zondervan. All rights reserved worldwide. www.zondervan.com. Scripture quotations marked (ESV) are taken from The Holy Bible, English Standard Version, copyright © 2001 by Crossway Bibles, a division of Good News Publishers. Used by permission. All rights reserved.

Italics in Scripture quotations reflect the author's added emphasis.

Details in some anecdotes and stories have been changed to protect the identities of the persons involved.

"We Live" lyrics used by permission of Alfred Music. Words and music by Jörgen Bo Fredriksson and Staffan Erik "Bosson" Olsson. Copyright © 2001 Warner/Chappell Music Scandinavia AB (Stim), M N W Music (Stim), and Emi Blackwood Music Inc. All rights on behalf of Warner/Chappell Music Scandinavia AB and M N W Music administered by WB Music Corp. All rights reserved.

Trade Paperback ISBN 978-1-60142-520-1
Hardcover ISBN 978-1-60142-519-5
eBook ISBN 978-1-60142-521-8

Copyright © 2014 by Anna Whiston-Donaldson

Cover design by Kristopher K. Orr

The photo on page 221 is by Kim Jackson.

Published in the United States by Convergent Books, an imprint of the Crown Publishing Group, a division of Penguin Random House LLC, New York.

CONVERGENT BOOKS® and its open book colophon are registered trademarks of Penguin Random House LLC.

The Library of Congress has cataloged the hardcover edition as follows:
Whiston-Donaldson, Anna.
    Rare bird : a mother's story of unthinkable loss, impossible hope, and a beautiful boy who flew too soon / Anna Whiston-Donaldson.—First Edition.
        pages cm
    ISBN 978-1-60142-520-1—ISBN 978-1-60142-521-8 (electronic) 1. Children—Death—Religious aspects—Christianity. 2. Mothers—Religious life. 3. Grief—Religious aspects—Christianity. 4. Bereavement—Religious aspects—Christianity. I. Title.
    BV4907.W46155 2014
    248.8'66092—dc23
    [B]
2014006689

2015—First Trade Paperback Edition

147468846

For Margaret and Tim. Red, yellow, blue...I love you!

contents

foreword

I have been praying for Anna and her family since Jack died, but my prayers are different than you might expect. My prayers sound less like "Help them" and more like "Help them. And please help me find the strength and faith that they have. Help me *mother* like Anna does. Help me *believe* like she does. Help my son learn what her son knew. Help my daughters trust God and persevere like Anna's daughter does."

Jack's death terrified me. I had so many selfish thoughts, such as, *If this could happen to Anna's Jack, that means it could happen to my Chase. How would I survive being separated from my only son?* At Jack's service, Anna started teaching me that love is bigger than fear. Anna started teaching me that even in the end, Love Wins. But I wondered—could it last? Could Anna's strength and hope withstand the onslaught of the coming days, months, and years without Jack?

After reading *Rare Bird,* I am done wondering. Oh, this book! Anna's storytelling is raw and real and intense and funny. Her voice is so comforting and accessible that all her wisdom and beauty and insight just sneaks in. And Anna's writing just *glimmers;* it somehow has *light in it.* This book took my breath away, but when I put it down, I felt able to breathe more deeply than I could before. *Rare Bird* made more space inside of me. Because through Anna's writing, my deepest fears were wrapped in a blanket of peace. It's true: nothing—not even death—ends the love between a mother and a son or the love between Father God and His daughter.

Jack's service was as brutal and beautiful as you might imagine, times infinity. The pastor said that in his thirty year career, he'd never seen his sanctuary so full. Most of the guests—children, adults, teens, elderly—wore teeny Lego cross pins. We gathered quietly with tissues and red eyes, and we did our best to hold space for the grief, confusion, and anger that threatened to swallow us all up. We were very, very lost. And then, in the middle of the service, we witnessed a miracle. Anna stood in front of the masses of mourners, and just days after her son's death, she delivered a flawless, tearless, divinely inspired tribute to Jack and to the power of faith. I have never seen anything braver or more exceptional in my life.

Anna did not allow death to stop her from honoring her son. Trusting God to help her, she stood and she spoke boldly and with truth and hope, and her voice did not quiver, not once. In the midst of her pain, she proved true her boy's belief that *nothing is impossible with God.* The congregation witnessed that scripture become real. And we needed scripture to become real, because after Jack's death, many of us felt a crisis of faith. Many of us had spent the previous days shaking furious fists at God and then doubting God's very exist-ence. Many of us walked into that memorial with less faith than we'd ever had in our lives. We'd shown up to comfort Anna, to hold *her* up, but she turned the tables.

As I watched her up there—strong, steady, and full of grace—I thought: *Anna is a Mother, capital M. I am witnessing the essence, the transcendent power of motherhood. It seems, somehow, that Jack's death has not robbed Anna of her role as his mother, but intensified it. Capitalized it. Anna is proving that nothing can separate us from the Love of our Father or from the Love for our children.*

Anna mothered not just Jack, but all of us at that service. She comforted *us,* she strengthened *our* faith, she ministered to *us* in her darkest hour. I don't think Anna set out to do all of that. I think she just *refused to quit mothering her boy.* Jack was Anna's miracle, so she honored him by performing a miracle of her own. I will never forget her miracle as long as I live. I will never forget her regal posture, her visible resolve, the mixture of tenderness and toughness in her face. Anna, standing on that stage, will forevermore be my mental image of *Mother.* Right beside Mary.

Anyone who needs to believe that her God is bigger than her fear needs to read this book. Everyone who is diving for treasure in the midst of life's wreck-age needs to read this book. EVERYONE needs to read *Rare Bird*. I plan to keep copies in my house to pass out to everyone who knocks on my door. *Rare Bird* is a masterpiece of hope, love, and the resilience and ferocity of the human spirit.

So read on, Lucky Bird.

Glennon Doyle Melton, founder of Momastery.com

introduction

You're Braver than You Think

I thought the first book I'd write would be about painting furniture. It would have suggestions, techniques, and even inspirational Bible verses sprinkled throughout it. It would have steps to follow so you could get your project done quickly and start enjoying it right away, because life is short and who knows how much longer the color persimmon will be in style? I'd share that just as I see little point in bothering with the back of my hair, painting the back of a dresser is not a requirement. The book would be simple, real, and hopefully funny.

That's the book I thought I'd write.

But this is the book I wrote. I wish I had nothing to say on the matter of loss, but I do. Because one ordinary day I encouraged my two kids to go out and play in the rain and only one child came home. I learned in that moment what many other people already knew: that it can all turn to shit in a heartbeat. All of it. Our families. Our futures. Our dreams. Even our faith.

And I went from being an ordinary mom, who blogged a lot about painting furniture and a little about my family and God, to someone who couldn't even recognize her own life anymore. The simple rhythm of my former days of shuttling kids around, helping them blossom into the people God made them to be, and trying to protect them from all kinds of danger now seemed like a cruel joke.

My new story was a tragedy so frightening that, as parents, we feel we risk something even by thinking about it, because it whispers into our hearts a truth we don't want to hear. That we can't keep our children safe. That we don't know what the future holds. We want to cover our ears, close our eyes, and turn away from the horror of that truth.

And it may be how you are feeling right now—you might be tempted to run away from this book. I get that. I do. Because we worry. In fact, I considered worry to be my job, and in my fear I wielded worry as a talisman to ward off danger and pain.

But this isn't a scary book. It's a book about a loving relationship between a mother and her boy. It's about being faced with impossible circumstances and wanting to accept nothing less than the chance to turn back the clock. It's about anger and profound sadness, but also about a flicker of hope that comes from the realization that in times of heartbreak, God is closer than our own skin. It's about being real and showing up in the pain.

And it's about surprises. The strange and creative ways God comforts us through signs and nature in ways I formerly would have considered either coincidences or desperate grasping. It's about mystery, such as why God would choose to comfort us so personally in our pain, but not choose to do the one thing we wanted Him to do, which was to save us from the pain in the first place.

It's about nudges and warning signs and the wisdom of a little boy. It's about how God and my son showed me—a buttoned-up, rule-following Christian—that I needed a bigger God. I needed the God of the universe who somehow held a plan in His hand—a plan for the ages, a plan that I hated— that went far beyond my meager understanding. Because my God of rules and committee meetings and sermon notes and praise music wasn't going to be enough for pain this big.

It's about matters as spiritual as heaven and angels, and as earthy as trying to give a damn again about marriage, sex, and recycling when just living through the day seems to be asking far too much.

So it's about contrasts. Feeling so utterly alone, yet somehow being connected to a larger community and the entire world. Being filled with grace while fighting off creeping bitterness. Feeling peace inside when any idiot can see that your life is destroyed. Needing people more than ever, but not knowing if your relationships can withstand the assault of grief.

It's about being connected in partnership with my son to share an ordinary family's story that there's more to this life than getting ahead and raising successful kids, and there's more to the afterlife than going someplace far "over there" while we are left behind here.

By coming alongside me, as I grapple with love and loss, I hope you'll realize that you're braver than you think and that survival *is* possible when life's storms take us in uncertain, unwanted directions, whether we're facing the loss of health, relationships, expectations, or even our dreams. And that with God we can do the impossible, while still honoring the tender spots where the pain is dulled but won't ever be forgotten.

I was just a mom with a paintbrush until I lost Jack. I'd give anything in this world to trade any wisdom or understanding I've gained just to have him back. I once thought my first book would be about color samples, and then I thought it would be about the loss of our beautiful son. But now I think maybe it's more of a universal story than I realized. The story of a woman who has suffered profound, crushing disappointment, whose plan didn't pan out, whose heart has been broken by life, and who is wondering if she's alone in her pain.

I

the storm

one

J ack and Margaret stand next to the table on a spring evening in 2011, looking out the kitchen's bay window as I finish cooking dinner. It's taco night. Tim will be home in a few minutes, then Margaret and I will head off in one direction for soccer, he and Jack in another for baseball.

"They're trying to fly!" Margaret exclaims, and she and Jack step closer to the window. My children are watching three baby cardinals gain the strength and skill to fly.

Every winter and spring we follow "our flock" of downy woodpeckers, cardinals, chickadees, and titmice as they rest on the bushes, eat from our feeders, and entertain us from this window. But this is the first spring we've seen an actual nest in the bushes and have watched baby birds hatching, and now this.

Yesterday a black snake inched its way up the bush, heading toward the nest where the still flightless babies sat. If it got to them, they wouldn't stand a chance. Amid both kids' screams, Tim ran out the door and chased the snake away with a broom. If these birds can get their act together and learn how to fly rather than continue their little hopping dance on our brick walkway, we think they'll have a pretty good chance of survival. It's what we're rooting for.

And today it happens. One by one, the fledglings figure out what they were born to do. The hopping morphs into something else entirely, and the tiny birds take flight. We gasp at the sight of a miracle.

Ten-year-old Margaret reaches around her big brother and gives him a squeeze, leaving her arm at rest on his back. He keeps looking out the window and says with a slight shake of his head, "They just grow up so fast." I laugh as they stand there like proud parents, Jack at twelve saying words that could so easily come out of my mouth.

Not that the twelve years of mothering these kids have gone by all that fast. In fact, some of the hardest, most relentless days felt a whole lot longer than just twenty-four hours. Like the many days when Tim worked nonstop—with a full-time job and then law school at night—and I had to figure out how to keep the kids occupied and myself sane until bedtime. There were days when I would plot to keep Jack and Margaret distracted just long enough to go to the bathroom without someone on my lap. There was my adjustment from being a busy high school English teacher to someone just hoping to catch the highlights in *People* magazine in the checkout line during a late-night solitary grocery store run.

Those were hard, good years. I tried to mother Jack and Margaret the way I had been mothered, with a lot of laughter, acceptance, and patience. Some days were disasters; others small, precious victories. And motherhood seemed to get easier as the years passed. When the kids were seven and nine, I began blogging about thrifty decorating projects and funny observations about family life. I hoped that an honest look at our experiences might give encouragement to other moms and help form a community for me.

Tim eventually scaled back his grueling career, choosing time with the family over money. He was able to coach baseball, lead Cub Scouts, and help with the church youth group we had formed. I started working part-time as the manager of our church bookstore after almost nine years at home, and we found a new rhythm that worked for us, much of it taking place by this bay window at the same round kitchen table from my childhood. In a way, Jack is right, they do grow up so fast, because even though the individual days sometimes felt dreadfully long, I'm baffled as to how we got to this place so soon.

I'll revisit this tender moment at the window a few weeks later, in early June, when it's time to read something to Jack at his sixth-grade graduation dinner from the kids' small private school. Tim and I will stand in front of Jack's friends and their parents in the back room of an Olive Garden, each with a hand on his shoulder. We'll look down into his deep brown eyes. I'll tell this story of the fledgling cardinals, ending with, "Jack, parenting you is an honor and a privilege, and we know the day is coming soon when you'll be flying on your own. When things get hard, and they will, please remember your special

Bible verse: *'For nothing is impossible with God.'* We are proud of you, Jack, and we love you very much." He'll smile an embarrassed smile, and I'll hope he hears, really hears, how proud we are of him. I'll give his shoulder an extra squeeze and steer him back to our seats.

As we twirl our pasta and bite into our breadsticks, we cannot know that three months later our son will indeed be flying on his own, not to middle school and the blossoming independence we had envisioned, but to someplace entirely different. And that in exactly three months, we would need to cling to his special Bible verse more than he ever did.

two

The small square photo with the white border curls up at the edges. In it, my sister, Liz, and I stand in the yard wearing long 1970s dresses with pinafores, fat yarn bows tying the ends of our french braids. Our brother, John, wears a plaid suit—polyester, of course—his white-blond hair sticking up with a major case of bed head on a chilly Virginia morning. Liz and John smile directly at the camera. My face is only visible from the side, because I'm looking away from the camera right at the contents of my older siblings' Easter baskets.

I don't remember living the moment captured in the photo, when I was maybe five years old, but I instantly recognize the feeling of wanting to make sure things were fair. Of sizing things up. Of caring an awful lot about the equitable distribution of chocolate bunnies and jellybeans. Of trying to figure out where I stood in the pecking order.

As a child, I was bookish and rule oriented, witty but tightly wound. I tried to be the best daughter, student, and Christian I could, always hoping to win brownie points in life. "Talking to you is like talking to an adult," I remember a friend saying to me when I was about eleven. I'm pretty sure it wasn't a compliment.

At only eighteen months older, Liz was my nemesis. She was smart, beautiful, and athletic. She seemed carefree, and to her, rules were more like suggestions than edicts. That rankled me. Shouldn't I be rewarded for doing all the right things, and shouldn't she be punished for, well, just about everything? It didn't seem fair. I would help around the house unasked, but I did it more to prove how good I was than to lift my mother's burden. Liz would do whatever she could to get out of helping. As the oldest, and the only boy, John pretty much escaped my rivalry and my wrath by lying low, occasionally shining his attention down on me by way of ruffling my hair or threatening me with a wedgie.

When Liz did anything wrong, I'd be quick to point it out, thinking this would somehow build me up. Once I even rang the next-door neighbors' doorbell to inform the quiet, older couple, "Liz picks her boogers and eats them!" For some reason, they gave me strange looks, and I walked home, perturbed.

I wanted to live in a world that made sense to me, with neat lines and graphs and deposits and withdrawals. I kept my side of the room neat. I could find my shoes. My homework sheets were uncrumpled. I did not want to live in a world where good things happened to "bad people." And in my protected early eighties suburban life as a preteen with an unfortunate Dorothy Hamill haircut and a sister who for some reason got to look like Farrah Fawcett, I thought I knew who should land squarely in the "bad" category.

Dad worked nonstop in those days, building his dental practice, so it was Mom who set the tone in our big old farmhouse plopped down on an acre in the middle of a subdivision of small split-levels and colonials. She's the one who let us barricade the windows and have tennis-ball battles in John's room. Who raced with us to see who would be the first one to dip a finger into a fresh jar of Peter Pan peanut butter. Who sat cross-legged on the kitchen counter listening to us talk about our days. Who hugged us to her soft chest when words weren't enough. Who accepted us no matter what. Who let us play in the rain.

She was the one who saw my constant striving and one day, looking up from a magazine at the kitchen table, said, "Anna, you need to relax. You try too hard." I knew she was right. Spending so much energy trying to avoid making mistakes and gain favor was exhausting, and it didn't make my life any better, only more stressful. She helped me begin to be less serious, to embrace my humor, admit my flaws, and focus more on living life than on trying to make sure everything was fair.

Mom created a home that felt loving, safe, and fun. Her steady faith in God showed us there was something solid to trust, something that went way beyond whatever circumstances we found ourselves in. We saw this as she relaxed into the life she'd been given.

I figured I'd have a lifetime to learn from my mother. But on a hot May day, when I was eighteen years old and home from college, I walked down a long hospital hallway to sounds of her crying out in pain. She had suffered a brain hemorrhage six weeks earlier, recovered almost completely at home, and was now back in the hospital because it had happened again. We'd talked on the phone that morning, laughing and joking, and she sounded just like herself. Today's visit was supposed to be nothing unusual—I'd brought along some art books to entertain her and a bulky camera to take pictures—but when I entered her room, it was clear she was in serious trouble. She was having another hemorrhage. I reached out for her small, smooth hand and prayed silently that she would be okay. I wanted to do something, to fight for her—the most important person in my world—but I felt weak and scared and vulnerable. I was still holding her hand a few hours later when she died.

The woman who could put anyone at ease and make all situations better, who could wield a monkey wrench, jump-start a car, soothe my anxious mind, and help me enjoy life, died right in front of me, and I didn't know what to do.

How could I possibly live without a mother, *my* mother? After spending only a few more minutes with her body, I walked down the cold hospital hallway toward the parking garage and caught a glimpse of myself in the glassed-in walls of the smoking lounge. I was just an ordinary girl in a surf shop T-shirt and jean skirt, about to exit the building a motherless daughter.

The petty concerns of my youth fell away from me like scales from my eyes. I now had a bitter answer to all my childhood striving: life wasn't fair, it would never be fair, and there was nothing I could do about it.

I kept my feelings inside. I could think of no other option than lacing up my K-Swiss sneakers and going forward despite the pain, trying to live a good life that would honor my mother and hopefully bring me a family of my own someday. A family to love in the same open, steady way she loved us.

Soon, I was back at college and then grad school, eventually meeting and falling in love with a dark-haired biology major over hikes, cheesy TV shows, and games of pool. I don't know if it was the perk of free movie rentals, since I was a part-time video store employee, my permed hair, or my status as an "older woman"—by all of six months—that attracted Tim to me. But I do know I found his gentle personality and even-keel demeanor irresistible. It also didn't hurt that he was easy on the eyes and liked to cook. He was thoughtful and made me smile. Tim and I complemented each other from the beginning, with my more outgoing, social personality and his quiet one. And while I may have seemed like his opposite in some ways, we both loved order and structure and shared the same simple goals: to work hard, live lives of integrity, and have a family. Almost five years later, we were married.

And as it turned out, my adult life really didn't look all that different from that of my childhood. Tim, Jack, Margaret, and I lived off of a quiet cul-de-sac only three miles from the old farmhouse where I grew up. The Presbyterian church where my seeds of faith grew and flourished was now the center of our spiritual lives and friendships; I even worked there while the kids were in school. I bought my groceries from Elmer, the same grocery store checker who had loaded paper bags into my mother's cart so many years before. Even Shadow, our smelly, goofy chocolate Lab, looked like the dogs of my childhood.

And though I'd traveled extensively in college and graduate school and appreciated the world beyond our town, I wasn't looking for any more excitement, drama, or adventure. Instead, I craved the simple rituals and sense of family I'd experienced in childhood and had grown to appreciate even more as I got older. Secret codes, inside jokes, and potty humor, even at the dinner table. The knowledge that people were more important than money, things, or getting ahead. Hanging out on a screened porch, playing charades, splashing around in puddles. Handing a sweaty kid a dripping Popsicle on a blistering July day. Singing vacation Bible school songs. Praying together every night.

Drawing from my mother's example, I'd learned to relax enough to be a fun mom, while still operating within the rules and structure that made me feel safe. By the time I became a mother at age twenty-nine, I had the life I wanted, even though I'd experienced enough grief and disappointment by then to know that life was not easy and that I don't get to choose how it all goes down.

But maybe some lessons need to be learned more than once. Because somewhere deep down, I guess I figured that losing my mother was enough. That I'd more than paid my dues. That choosing to embrace a positive life instead of sinking into bitterness and despair should count for something. Deep down, maybe I was still that little girl with the Easter basket trying to control every outcome and make sure things were fair.

three

I wonder if I should have felt it coming. When something enormous is afoot, is there a rumbling in the earth, does the air feel different? I look back, searching my memories of that final summer for clues. And now I see them there: sign after sign after sign. I just didn't realize it at the time.

What about when the kids returned from church camp in late July and Margaret asked God to show her a special Bible verse to guide her life? Jack had discovered Luke 1:37 in fourth grade: "For nothing is impossible with God." I'm not sure if he picked it as his favorite because of its brevity or because it encouraged him in the challenges he faced.

As Margaret prayed in her room, the words *Isaiah 43:1–2* came clearly into her mind. Isaiah 43:1–2. What? Who knew if there were even such verses in the Bible? She looked them up, hoping to find something inspirational and applicable to her young life, not something scary about casting out demons or gross like circumcision. Here's what she found:

> Fear not, for I have redeemed you;
>> I have summoned you by name; you are mine.
> When you pass through the waters,
>> I will be with you;
> and when you pass through the rivers,
>> they will not sweep over you.
> When you walk through the fire,
>> you will not be burned;
>> the flames will not set you ablaze.

She wrote it in cursive on a fancy notecard and hung it on her mirror. After showing it to me, she said, "I like these verses, but now I'm worried it means I'm going to have to go through really hard things in life, and I don't want to." Such wisdom from a girl barely ten years old. I told her that everyone goes through *some* hard things, but that she'd never have to face them alone. God would be with her. Thinking of my healthy family and our simple yet stable lives, it was hard to imagine Jack or Margaret having to experience anything more dramatic or difficult than just coasting through the final weeks of what had been a beautiful summer.

Then it was finally time for our annual August beach trip to North Carolina. After six hours in the car, we pulled up to a miniature-golf range, which was decked out in some sort of Wild West prospector theme. Minigolf was our cue that we had "arrived" at the beach. The previous year's golf outing had been a disaster. The sun beat down on us, showing no mercy, causing sweat to pool where it shouldn't. The pirate theme was lame, our games were off, our family barely tolerable. By the time we'd made it to the eighth hole, I was ready to make Tim, Margaret, and Jack walk the plank. I was even annoyed with myself. I wanted air conditioning, iced tea, and somewhere private to mop up my under-boob area.

This year had an equally inauspicious beginning. Margaret was cranky after the long drive. She was complaining about something as we gathered our things and got out of the car. *Snap!* Somehow she managed to break Tim's sunglasses in two. The four of us stood by the car, looking at one another. Our family dynamics were fairly predictable. Twelve-year-old Jack's face would fall. He would clamp his lips together in frustration, knowing there'd be no minigolf today. Tim would yell, and Margaret would cry and try to turn it back on him. I'd be mad at Tim for being too harsh, Margaret for being irresponsible, and Jack for being so disappointed about the aborted mission. I mean, it's only minigolf! Both parents would catastrophize, "Why can't we ever do something fun like normal people?" We'd get right back into the car and drive the rest of the way to the beach house fuming in silence.

Instead, this is how it went: "You need to buy me new sunglasses!" Tim growled, and Margaret said, "How much were these?" Jack and I held our breath, expecting to hear something like, "Fifty dollars," followed by Margaret's screechy wailing. "Twelve dollars," Tim answered in a calm, nongrowly voice. "Okay," she said, in a calm, nonwaily voice. "Sorry, Dad."

And with that, we locked the car and headed to play golf, surprising ourselves. I felt a cool breeze, which came either from the refreshing experience of a family crisis averted or from picking a much better day for minigolf. We laughed. Tim and I didn't argue over our scores. No one threw a ball or a stubby little wooden pencil, and no one stomped around. I did not hide in a cheesy faux mine shaft seeking a little alone time. Afterward, Tim sprung for overpriced cups of frozen lemonade instead of saying, "Let's wait and buy ice cream at the grocery store."

We lined up on a wooden bench, the kids swinging their legs and scraping their lemonade with little wooden spoons. Jack said in his lightning-fast speech, best understood by family and close friends, "You know there are two courses here. We did Gold. Want to do Platinum now?" I looked at my family. Smiling. Happy. "Let's not push it," I said. He looked at me and nodded with a knowing little smile, and then we headed back to the car.

We'd started vacationing at the beach with close friends when the kids were two and four, and each summer it had gotten easier and better. During the early years, when we stayed in beach rentals that weren't babyproofed, every loose venetian blind cord, sliding glass door to the ocean, and rickety, splintery deck seemed like a death trap. We rented houses with pools and hot tubs, which terrified me and put me on high alert for our kids, and those of our friends. Throw in the whining, picky eating, and disrupted sleep schedules, and sometimes we wondered why we bothered at all. It seemed like an awful lot of work.

Now, with a ten- and twelve-year-old, we could relax, watching from deck chairs while the kids swam in the pool. We played cards and other games at night. Mind-numbing Candy Land had blessedly given way to Monopoly, Settlers of Catan, and Pictionary. Bedtimes weren't a struggle anymore, and we could go on day trips with just the four of us. Our beach vacations were never lavish—the whole reason we went in August was because the rental rates dropped so much—but they were a way to make memories that we could draw on throughout the year. This bolstered my sense of family, which had inescapably felt cut off and broken after my mom's death.

We liked to set up an extra table so Tim and Jack could work on a jigsaw puzzle throughout the week. This year Jack had the chance to sleep downstairs in a bunk room with the two other boys, children of our dearest friends, but instead he chose to stay upstairs and share a room with Margaret. This was one of his favorite parts of being at the beach, dating back to when Margaret was barely out of a Pack 'n Play. He'd tell her all sorts of facts in the dark about whatever interested him at the time, whether it was trains, mythology, or baseball, and then quiz her on them until she'd fall asleep in the middle of a question.

I wasn't sure whether it would be awkward for them to share a bed at this age, with Jack about to enter seventh grade, so I set up a blow-up mattress for him just in case. They hung out in their room watching the Little League World Series on TV, and they saw a show called *Ghost Hunters* for the first time. That night after prayers, Jack, from his mattress on the floor, started talking about the ghost show. Within seconds, Margaret was freaked out and crying, and Jack crawled up into the bed to comfort her. This rendered the question of separate sleeping areas moot, and Jack stayed in the big bed with her for the whole trip.

For years I reasoned that because I was primarily a stay-at-home mom, the beach was my time to relax away from the kids, thereby generously providing Tim with time to catch up with them. I lobbied to stay inside, under the covers in the daytime, working my way through a delicious pile of books on the bedside table, emerging now and then to visit under a beach umbrella, reapply the kids' sunscreen, supervise pool time, or eat a bowl of ice cream.

Tim always rose to the occasion, and he'd become known as a master sandcastle builder, pool playmate, hole digger, and an acceptable kite flyer. He worked hard at his job, but when he was with the kids, he was truly with them.

Sometimes I'd feel a teeny bit bad that Tim was so creative and fun, when I seemed to veer toward tired and grumpy. When they were tiny, he could take them to the zoo with nothing but one diaper and a ten-dollar bill in a backpack, and they'd have a fabulous time. I'd think of all the snacks and sunscreen and parking stubs and sippy cups and changes of clothes I'd need for that kind of outing and, more often than not, talk myself into staying home with them and letting them run through the sprinkler with their clothes on instead. I reasoned that he was on a sprint, pulling out all the stops during the times he could be with the kids, and I was on a marathon and therefore needed to pace myself.

Our friends' children loved boogie boarding and playing in the waves, but Jack and Margaret stayed on the sand, going down to the water's edge only to refill a bucket or let the foam splash over their feet. Jack, in particular, did not like the mighty power of the ocean. He was such a cautious boy. No amount of coaxing could get him to go in, so we had quit trying years before. It might seem strange that our favorite vacation spot was the beach, considering neither child went in the water. But they loved digging and building in the sand with Tim. These North Carolina beaches were known for occasionally having dangerous rip currents, so I was relieved to have one less thing to fret about. I'd never have to worry about my kids being swept away.

Jack's summer assignment for their small Christian school was to read and annotate *Oliver Twist*. Not an abridged version, but the whole shebang. As a former high school English teacher, I knew this would be a challenge for most high school or college students, not to mention twelve-year-olds. Jack read chunks here and there but did not barrel through it. He carried the thick book with him wherever we went that summer, reading a little bit here and there.

The week prior to going to the beach, I checked out the audio version, which consisted of thirteen disks, from the library as backup. Within a few minutes of listening to it in the car, Jack began laughing uncontrollably. He held his chest with his hands and heaved up and down in his seat. I asked him what was so funny. He could barely speak. "Play it again!" Gasp. "Play it

again!" We replayed the section in question. Turns out there's a young charac-
ter named Charley Bates, who is referred to four times in a row as "Master
Bates." Master Bates. Hysterical stuff to a twelve-year-old boy. Problem was,
Margaret was in the car too. I had a little explaining to do. Teachable moment,
I guess. After that we ditched the audio book in favor of Jack reading silently.

Tim grew increasingly worried that Jack wouldn't finish the book because
of how slowly and sporadically he was reading it. I assured Tim he would finish. It reminded me of how some adults cannot stand the stress of seeing a child
do the potty two-step—hopping from foot to foot—obviously having to pee,
but refusing to go. The anticipation and uncertainty are simply too much for
the observer to bear, and that person feels like he or she must step in.

Watching Jack pick up the book and languidly assure us he had the situation under control was tough on Tim and his desire to fix the situation. In our
parenting dance I was the one in favor of natural consequences and letting
them manage their own time. Tim was in favor of staying on top of the kids.
We both leaned toward parenting in the way we were raised.

I thought the fact that Tim had Jack doing handwriting improvement
exercises over the summer was about as much micromanaging as we needed.
But by the time we got to the beach in late August, I realized Tim was probably
right. Jack still had a long way to go in the book.

So Jack and I decided to read to each other in the afternoons, when the sun
was the harshest. We settled under the covers of the beach house's king-size
bed, sunlight streaming through the blinds. It reminded me of tender times in
middle school and high school when my mom and I would climb into my
parents' huge bed after church on Sundays, she in her long slip and me in a
dress, and read the *Washington Post* side by side until one of us fell asleep.

Jack handed me the well-worn piece of paper on which he'd been taking
notes, opened the book, and began to read to me. I'd stop him occasionally to
ask questions, because this book was full of intrigue and strange coincidences
and I didn't want to miss a thing. He'd fill me in on the intricacies of the plot,
and as we talked, I'd be once again amazed at him. Jack was so humble it was

easy for me to forget that the kinds of conversations we shared as mother and son were probably not commonplace. It felt good to put my own beach books aside and spend this time with him.

When Margaret wanted a break from the sun, she invoked her God-given right to shop. I dragged her into the small Hanes underwear outlet, and she helped me pick out my first new bras in years, finally retiring the ones that looked more like used jockstraps than bras. We discussed cup size, band size, and the all-important petal shield feature. Later, we drove to little shops to look at hermit crabs, buy fudge, and marvel at the volume of personalized key chains, license plates, and pens.

One day we sat in the living room of the beach house, in a relaxed, pre-dinner slump, and the house swayed a little. I was cruising Facebook on my phone, and I thought Tim must have been running up the stairs. Suddenly my news feed filled with a strange word: *earthquake.* We were expecting weird weather this week, having heard on the weather stations we would most likely be evacuated midweek because of an impending hurricane, but an earthquake? In North Carolina? That was just too strange. Hurricane? Earthquake? What was next? I wondered. Tsunami? The floor-to-ceiling windows let in tons of sunshine, and the ocean looked almost placid. No one else in the house had felt a thing. What was going on?

A few times on each beach trip, Tim would take the kids out again in the early evening, when the sun wasn't as harsh on their skin and they were the only ones left on the beach. I rarely joined them, but this year I did. I don't know why. Did I somehow know this would be our last time at the beach as a family of four?

Jack set up an elaborate game in the sand that would soon wash back into the sea, fading just like the memories of our final vacation before school began. He and Margaret explained the rules to Tim and me, and we all played, throwing globs of sand, attempting to knock sand royalty off the tops of their enormous castles. It wasn't easy. But instead of wandering off into my own thoughts as I normally would, I stayed in the moment, trying to knock the suckers into oblivion. When Jack hit one, he did something he called the "roll of glory," running down the beach with his arms in the air, then making a rolling dive into the sand. When he missed, it was the "roll of shame." In victory or defeat, sand filled his hair and ears and clung to his lightly browned neck.

Margaret's cheeks and nose were pink from the sun despite our best efforts with sunscreen, and she leaped through the sand like a ballerina and challenged me to a race. We walked back up to the house for a final night of card playing and trying to eat all the food in the fridge. We'd just found out we'd be evacuating to Virginia in the morning.

four

The next day the car slogged up I-95 with what seemed like the rest of the world, a caravan of minivans and SUVs packed high with coolers and sand toys. It was slow going. We'd obeyed the evacuation orders even though the beautiful blue skies and warm ocean water of late summer seemed to belie Hurricane Irene's existence. Tim switched off the weather report and plugged in his iPod. Jack read his book. I checked Facebook. Margaret fiddled with my camera, taking pictures and videos. Some of my favorite home movies are two-to-three-second clips of the kids acting weird in the backseat, contorting their faces and making up rhymes, funny only to each other.

On the drive we'd heard a lot of Jack's current favorite word: "butt." He collected words the way others might collect baseball cards. The words of this summer appeared to be "You betcha!" said with exaggerated enthusiasm, a cheesy smile, and a big thumbs-up, and the words "butt" or "my butt." He would mutter them under his breath or tack them onto sentences where they didn't apply at all. "Jack, do you want to go to the grocery store?"

"My butt. No thanks." Okay...Margaret and I found it hilarious, but we hoped he'd get it out of his system before school started, because we didn't think his teachers would look too kindly on "my butt" as a blanket response to questions.

I'd called a doctor about Jack's repetition of words over the past year or so. Was it a problem? Did he need help to stop saying them? "Nope," she said. "Jack just likes words. Hasn't he always?" "Well, yes." So we'd gotten used to his choosing a few words like "gorge," "zest," or "butt" and saying them at odd times until he and his friends grew tired of them and moved on to something else. It was just Jack being Jack.

And now, in the backseat, Margaret put down the camera and turned to face him.

"Jack, you're going to die young."

Up front, Tim and I barely registered what she was saying. Was this one of their games? Were they making another funny movie?

Jack looked up from his book and asked, "When?"

"Around fifteen."

Later, she and I will talk about this strange moment, relying on each other's memories to prove that such a thing had really happened, and she will admit she'd tacked on a few extra years so what she said wouldn't seem quite so terrible. She will say she had no idea why those words came into her head. Jack looked at her for a second, mumbled, "My butt," removed his finger from where he'd been marking his page, and began reading again.

A few hours later, we pulled into our driveway and Jack's friend Daniel raced up to the car. He was visiting his dad, who lived with his grandparents and uncle in the house that shared our driveway. Nearly a week apart had been too long for these fast friends who tried to spend every possible moment together. The boys had known each other since ages four and two, and they loved to play video games or games that Jack made up. Daniel went with us on family hikes and out to eat. A great day for Jack was what he called a "Daniel Day," meaning one of the frequent days Daniel was in the neighborhood.

When we rolled down our car window, Daniel spilled out some news in speech almost as fast as Jack's. "I'm moving in! I'm moving in! I'm even going to school here!" Although Daniel had been a big presence in our lives for years when he would come over, he lived with his mother about a half hour away. We weren't sure why he was moving in with his grandparents and father now, but this was big news, indeed.

Daniel's grandparents were like family to us, which was good because we lived practically on top of one another. Our street ended in a typical cul-de-sac, but with one long, narrow pipestem driveway veering off it to the right. Our two split-level houses faced each other at the very top of the pipestem, separated only by a strip of blacktop. For the past eight years, we had seen life unfold in each other's carports and front kitchen windows. Because of the shared driveway, there was no real delineation of where our property stopped and Clark and Donna's began. We had an easy, comfortable relationship of sharing canned goods and spices, picking up each other's mail and newspapers, and spending time together in the driveway on nice days.

Clark and Donna treated our kids like their own grandkids, buying them presents and giving them hugs. They even let our dog out for me while I was at work. Each spring, Donna's garden was full of tulips that she and Margaret planted together when Margaret was barely out of diapers. On the many days when Donna took care of her grandchildren, kids would run back and forth between our two houses all day long, kicking off their shoes inside each kitchen door, if they'd bothered to put any on in the first place.

Sometimes Jack would be so excited to see Daniel motioning to him from one kitchen window to the other at breakfast time that he'd pull clothes on right over the top of his pj's and run out the door.

Now, Jack and Margaret climbed out of the car and ran off to catch up with Daniel and their other friends in the cul-de-sac at the bottom of the driveway and get reacquainted with the Virginia mosquitoes, while Tim and I launched into our well-choreographed unpacking routine. I never really felt we were "home" until all the vacation stuff was put away, and I wondered how less than a week out of town could yield such a massive mound of crap.

"Did you feel that?" I asked Tim as we both leaned into the back of the car, reaching for bags and laundry baskets.

"Feel what?"

"Ugh at Daniel's news?" It felt as though a pound of lead had settled in the pit of my stomach and something was pushing my shoulders toward the earth.

"Yeah," he answered, our eyes meeting, a serious look on his face.

I tried to lighten the mood. "This will *not* end well," I said to Tim with a

small laugh as we unpacked, using the phrase the kids and I saved for some of
our most ill-fated adventures. I sensed that having Jack's buddy Daniel around
all the time would bring changes, but I wasn't sure how.

A few nights later the hurricane finally reached our area, albeit with much less
severity than was anticipated at the beach. I felt uneasy and restless. I stayed up
all night in the family room, for some reason moved to pray specifically for
Jack, his safety, his friendships, and his future. Why wasn't I praying that massive trees wouldn't hit our house or that our basement wouldn't flood? I didn't
know. The next morning was sunny and beautiful, and we had no damage to
our house or yard. It felt good to have all that anticipation over, after more than
a week's warning. The big storm was behind us.

Fun on our street continued into the waning days of August with lemonade stands and bake sales on the corner as the neighborhood kids earned money
to turn Clark and Donna's old shed into a clubhouse. In only a few days, they'd
made enough to buy secondhand furniture and a small fridge at the thrift shop.
Soon the girls dubbed Jack "the Lawyer" as he tried to ease a conflict that
sprang up between Daniel, a new boy named Joe, and the girls.

Jack wanted everyone to get along, and he wasn't sure where he fit into the
equation. Before, he always knew his place was right at Daniel's side, but Daniel was splintering off with Joe to start a separate clubhouse in Joe's yard, and
Jack didn't want to join them. He was close to Margaret and all the girls. Besides, good friends when you are four can become girlfriends when you are
fourteen, and Jack didn't want to piss anyone off. Things were falling apart as
they do with kids. I was glad that school was about to start so the adolescent
drama could die down.

Finally, the last week of summer arrived. I could almost smell the scent of
school supplies in the air and taste the freedom of being able to work a full day
at the bookstore again without having to figure out what to do with the kids.

Jack began experiencing severe stomach pains. I let it go for a day or two. He went to pool parties with his school friends and said it hurt to swim, run around, and jump on the trampoline, so I decided to take him to the doctor. I thought he was probably fine, but what if his appendix burst and I'd just blown it off?

A team of three doctors examined him and ruled out anything serious. Then they got personal as they poked around his very ticklish midsection. Could it be a bowel issue?

"No!" Jack was adamant, as if the mere suggestion of his pain being poop related was an affront to his twelve-year-old dignity. Gross. "This has nothing to do with poo!" he insisted.

Alrighty, then.

One doctor tried a different approach, asking quietly, "Could it be stress?"

Jack answered softly, looking down, "Yes."

In bed that night, during our snuggle time in the dark, I asked Jack, "So you're feeling stressed?"

"Yes."

"About what?"

Silence.

"Is it Daniel and Joe?"

"Uh-huh. I just don't understand what's going on." But I did. To me it looked like a classic case of tastes and loyalties changing, spurred on by Joe moving into the neighborhood a few months earlier and Daniel moving in full-time just two weeks ago. The two younger boys would be going to school together, while Jack would be in middle school. Daniel and Joe had bonded while our family was away at the beach, so by the time Jack got home, things were different, and Jack could feel it.

I went through the same thing at Jack's age, when my friend Kendra Peters stopped calling me and threw me over for Cathy Simmons. It was my first heartbreak, and I could still remember the sting. I wasn't happy that Jack felt confused and left out, but I knew it was his nature to just hang back, say nothing, and see how this all unfolded. He wouldn't make a big deal of it. He would be fine.

I also knew that within a matter of days, Jack would be busy with church youth group, baseball, and hanging out with his middle school friends. This would provide the natural break that Tim and I anticipated, a transition to Jack spending more time with friends his own age.

And now, thank goodness, I finally understood the dread I'd been feeling since we returned from the beach. It wasn't Hurricane Irene. It wasn't Jack's appendix. Daniel had a new friend, and Jack felt like he was getting the shaft. I was relieved that this was all it was. *This too shall pass,* I thought.

Those last weeks of summer had God leading Margaret to a beautiful Bible verse about His protection of her during incredible hardships, and then there was Margaret's bizarre statement in the car about Jack dying young. There was Tim's and my physical sense of concern when we heard that Jack's good friend was moving in next-door, and Jack's own body telling him something was off. But just as the earthquake ended up causing little more than curiosity, and the much-hyped hurricane passed us by with no more than a whimper, we never anticipated that these strange, small things could portend a tragedy that would change our lives forever.

five

Summer's over. It's the second day of school, and Jack and Margaret sit at the table doing homework by candlelight. The power is out—we assume due to the heavy rain—and we're loving it. No electricity means unplugging as a family for a night of board games, spooky showers by candlelight, and most likely eating a lot of ice cream before it starts to soften.

Driving home from school a few minutes earlier had been an adventure, as we made our way through flooded streets that looked like a river of chocolate milk. We saw our favorite tiny pond overflowing its banks. We took a different route home because we assumed that the road outside our development that crossed over a small creek bed would probably be flooded. I was grateful to have a carport, because the three of us didn't get a single drop of rain on us as we made our way with backpacks and lunch bags into the house.

Compared to all the hype about the hurricane two weeks ago, this warm, windless rain doesn't strike us as threatening. I'll find out later that our friends around the corner set up a stadium tent to greet the kids at the elementary school bus stop with cupcakes, and that children and moms stood in the street talking, laughing, and getting soaked in the warm rain. It had rained on and off for days, ending summer fun a little bit early for Margaret and Jack, and leaving the soccer and baseball fields too soggy for practices.

I'm relieved the weather gives us a chance to ease back into our school year routine instead of being slammed by having to run all over town. We've heard no mention of extreme weather or flooding today. It's not until I leave my windowless office at the church to go pick up the kids from school at three that I even know the weather is dicey. It's not a thunderstorm, but a steady, heavy rain coming down in the steamy, sultry air.

Listening to Jack run through the best parts of his day in the car, we hear him use the word "bogus" four times. Margaret and I exchange glances and

smiles in the rearview mirror, noting with satisfaction that "butt" has been replaced by a more school-appropriate word. Thank you, Jack.

"Why did Dad take me to Legoland when I was twelve, not thirteen?"
Jack asks, out of nowhere. We had told the kids we would take them each
somewhere special when they turned thirteen, but frequent-flyer miles, a free
place to stay, and an admission coupon enabled Tim to take Jack to California
in March for his twelfth birthday instead. He had really wanted to go to Legoland in Denmark, but with our budget that wasn't realistic.

"Well, we saved a lot of money on that trip. Besides we didn't want to wait
until you were thirteen in case you wouldn't be interested in Legos anymore,"
I respond.

"But I'll never be too old for Legos!" Jack says, and I believe him.

Margaret pipes up, "Well, if it gives you a chance to save more money for
my trip, so it can be really good, you can wait until I'm thirteen." These kids
crack me up.

Right before we pull into our neighborhood, Jack tells us a funny story
about a skit he and his friend Davis made up that day in school. A skit? Jack
could make fun anywhere he went, but please tell me he and his friend did not
interrupt class time to launch into a skit! My eyes dart to the mirror again as I
sharply call, "Jack!"

I do not want my smart, charming kid to start seventh grade as a goof-off.
We'd had several touching bedtime talks over the summer about how he
wanted to be known as more serious this year, having his attitude match his
good grades.

"Stop, Mom, no!" his words come rushing out, in response to my exasper-
ated tone. "It wasn't like that at all. It was at indoor recess. This is going to be
the best year ever!"

And I know he is right. Not only is he caring and funny, but he has become comfortable in his own skin, which had been my greatest prayer since he
was a toddler. He has good friends and a strong moral compass, and he is ready
for the freedom and responsibility that will come in seventh grade.

Our plan was to make nachos for a snack—refried beans and cheese piled high on our plate of chips—but with no power for the microwave, that's a no-go. So I put out apple slices with peanut butter, and we talk about how great school is going so far, particularly how excited Jack is about English, science, and Bible classes. Margaret is excited about her new teacher, and both kids are thrilled to catch up with their friends again.

Homework done, Jack plays hide-and-seek with Shadow, our chocolate Lab, by hiding from her under her very own dog bed, while Margaret changes out of her school uniform into a yellow Snoopy shirt and red soccer shorts, then finishes her snack. It is almost five o'clock but very light and balmy outside. We are dry and content, with no plans to change that. Jack is disappointed he can't upload a photo of one of his Lego creations to enter it in a contest, because it is due today. No electricity. No computer. That means no Lego contest.

The rain picks up and a knock comes at our kitchen door. Daniel, Joe, and another friend, Alexis, soaked from walking home in the rain from the bus stop, ask if Jack and Margaret can come outside. A quick "Go for it!" from me and my kids are out the door. I don't know how many times I'd told them of the crazy fun my sister and I had tromping through the flooded dips and valleys of our own yard as kids, but I do know I had told them. I wish I had never told them.

My last sight of them is five soaked, happy kids walking down our driveway toward the cul-de-sac. Jack, still in his school uniform of navy polo and long khaki shorts, arms raised to the sky, does a full spin with a huge smile on his face, his little sister at his side.

Tired after my first full day of work in a while, I wonder how long it will take us to adjust to the back-to-school routine: the driving, the schlepping, the lunches, the homework. It seems like such a drag compared to the freedom of summertime, even though I had yearned for a return to structure and more alone time. I change out of my work clothes, crawl under the covers of my bed, and by the light of a camping lantern, read a magazine article about a family who left their affluent lives behind to live in an RV and serve the poor, city by city, in two-month stretches. I want that kind of meaning and impact for our family. But how?

Our family motto is "The Best Things in Life Aren't Things," but as I sit by the lantern light, I wonder how we can live that out in a more meaningful way. Sometimes I feel as though we are coasting through life, missing opportunities to really make a difference. We are well past the years of just survival mode, simply trying to hang on with babies and toddlers until bedtime. Couldn't we do something significant, serve the world, and get off the grid, all without killing one another?

Probably not, but I like the fantasy, so I fold down the page to share at dinnertime. I may hear thunder at this point. You know those parenting moments when you let something go on too long against your better judgment, but you do it anyway? It could be a play date that quickly turns to crap when your kid has a colossal meltdown just because you needed a little more adult time with the other mom, or a party you know you shouldn't let your teenage daughter go to, but you are too tired and fed up to deal with any more drama, tears, and arguing.

So if I do hear thunder, I don't really *listen*. I just don't know. I was known as the "Thunder Nazi" at sporting events, because when I was seventeen, a younger friend from church was struck and killed by lightning in his own front yard. I had no patience for Little League coaches who wanted to "just finish this inning" when we could all hear thunder. It just wasn't worth the risk.

I talk to Tim at his office and suggest we go out to dinner because the lights are out and we have no sports practices. It's rare to have a night without baseball. But we decide traffic will be awful and we'll just forage from the fridge when he gets home instead of getting caught out late on a school night. So I let the kids stay out longer, later, until just after six. After all, it's lighter and warmer outside than in.

Tim calls again, this time from the road, and says he saw lightning, and I hear thunder in earnest and immediately go to get the kids.

If Jack had a cell phone, I would text them, "Thunder. Come Home" at this point. But we haven't gotten around to buying him one. We aren't sure if he needs it since he has door-to-door service from school to home every day in my car and attends the same tiny school he has been in since first grade. Does he really need a phone, or does he just want one? Is Jack's assessment that "everybody in seventh grade has a phone" accurate? We are going to reevaluate our stance once school gets underway and I can talk to some of the other moms about it. We are also going to buy him new underwear and find his missing dictionary.

Even though the cul-de-sac is right at the bottom of our long driveway, I decide to take the car so I won't get soaked. What's fun when you are ten or twelve is not so much if you're forty-one. When I reach the cul-de-sac, it is empty. Have the kids gone into Alexis's or Joe's house? I look farther up the street and see Margaret walking slowly toward me. She'll tell me later she felt a strong urging that she should come home. I pull up to her and have her climb into the car. I ask where Jack is, and she replies calmly, "In Joe's backyard." She tells me Alexis had already gone home, so it's just the boys.

Not a single thought of our neighborhood's paltry little creek enters my mind at this point, only the danger of lightning. I park in front of Joe's house and wait a few seconds, wondering which gate to use. I have never been in his backyard before. I slowly step out of the car, harrumphing about having to go out in the rain.

six

As I enter the yard and call Jack's name, Joe's mom leans out the open rear window of her dining room, one story above me, and says, "Jack's not down there with them." Down where? I can't see any children in her yard. Does she mean by the neighborhood creek that joins the bottom of the steep backyards on this side of the street? Can she see the kids from where she is standing?

"Jack *is* with them. Margaret says he is," I respond. Who knows how long this exchange takes. Five seconds? More?

I still can't see because of the slope of the yard, but I can hear whoops of laughter of boys having fun below, and I quicken my pace down the steep stone steps built into the backyard that lead to woods and the creek. A creek with sheer, straight sides going more than five feet down to sandy, rocky soil and usually an inch or two of standing water. When I get to the bottom of the hill, I see just two boys, not three. I don't understand. I shout to Joe and Daniel, "Where's Jack?" and they answer, laughing and pointing, "In the river! In the river!"

"The *river?*" My God. Our crappy little creek is now a raging river with walls of rushing water barreling around a sharp curve, and Jack is gone! The boys must have no concept of how serious this is. Downstream I see nothing but white water. How late am I? One second? Ten? A minute? It cannot have been more than that. I was so close! What happened down here while I'd been talking to Joe's mom at the top of the hill? Why had she thought Jack wasn't in her yard? Does that mean she had watched the kids go down to the creek?

I don't know how I know, standing at the water's edge, that Jack is gone forever. How does one shift gears so suddenly, from brightly calling out your kid's name on a carefree afternoon to realizing with horror that he is dead or dying? I imagine Mack trucks would make a noise if they tried to shift gears so abruptly, but for me it is a silent scream, a terrible knowing that slams physically down on my body. I don't know how I know at that second that Jack will die, but I do.

"Look for him!" I scream at the boys and take off running. Shouting Jack's name, I run through the woods along the creek's edge. I lose my flip-flops in the underbrush and struggle to hold up my rain-soaked sweatpants as I fight through branches and briars. One misstep at the edge and I'll fall off the sheer sides into the water and be swept away. I have the feeling that Jack is already gone. That *no one* could survive what I am seeing.

This looks nothing like the kind of creek where you would toss in rocks to make a splash, roll up your pant legs and wade in, or watch bugs or dried leaves skim across the water. Nothing. My brain hurts. How could I go from casually calling out my perfectly healthy son's name, so he would come in out of the rain, to desperately searching for any sign of him? I feel a sense of hopelessness rising within me. I want to sit in the grass and cover my head with my hands. But this is my child, so my self-talk goes something like *"Don't give up, Anna! Don't give up. Jesus,* HELP *me. DON'T GIVE UP!"*

Truthfully, I can't see how a seventy-pound child could survive even a few horrifying seconds in that current, a current that I'd find out later was making two-thousand-pound cars bob along the roads. This piddly creek was the same creek that had flooded the road outside our neighborhood just three hours before, and since then it has been rising by the second. Jack is not a strong swimmer, and I don't see how even an Olympian could survive the power and force I see in front of me. I run up through another backyard and yell for a neighbor's girlfriend to call 911, and I ask a neighbor to look for Jack. Then I run back to the car. I don't know where the other two boys are at this point.

"What's going on?" Margaret asks from the backseat, panic in her voice.

"Jack fell in the creek!" I yell. She immediately starts to wail. I want to comfort her and help her not be afraid. "It's okay! It's okay! We're going to find him!" I shout as I try yet fail to stay calm. It's clear to me that with the force of the water, Jack is already well past our neighborhood, and I know in my soul I

must get down to the flooded section of the two-lane road, where this rushing
water leads. I know I have to get to the place outside our neighborhood that
we'd had to drive around earlier in order to get home. The creek narrows considerably there and grows shallow where there's a small wooden footbridge and
two large metal drainpipes that run under the paved road.

I speed out of our neighborhood, driving barefoot, with Margaret in the
backseat. Traffic on one side of the road is stopped because of the flooding, so
I start driving the wrong way down the two-lane road, honking my horn at
oncoming cars, hoping to make it to where I somehow know we will find Jack.
I don't get far because I become fearful. I start to doubt myself. Can this really
be happening? What if someone crashes into us? If I abandon Margaret and
the car on the road so I can run to the bridge on foot, what will happen to her?
She seems so small and scared. My behavior seems so rash. So strange.

Barely out of our neighborhood, and not even one-tenth of a mile from
where I think Jack will be, I make a split-second decision to turn back, driving
through someone's yard, leaving deep ruts in the grass. My crazy driving frightens Margaret even more, and I yell again, "It's going to be okay!" My voice
sounds fierce and desperate. A sickening thought flickers in my brain, the
thought that I am *choosing*. Choosing to comfort and keep safe the child in my
care and turn away from the one I cannot see. None of this feels real.

I feel I know exactly where Jack is but cannot get to him. But do I really
know? And *why* would I even know if I'm not able to get there and do something about it? We pull back into our neighborhood, parking in front of Joe's
house. I call 911 on my cell phone, growing angry when the operator tells me
to calm down. I hate her.

As I drop Margaret off at my friend Kristen's house next-door to Joe's, I
hand her my cell phone and say, "Call Daddy." She dials, then hands the phone
to Kristen, too upset to speak. I go outside to wait for help to arrive.

After telling Tim that Jack is lost in the creek, my friend prays silently,
hugging Margaret, saying again and again, "They're going to find him."

Tim is still on his way home from work, delayed by the traffic and flooding, when he gets the call. He immediately calls his friend John and asks for prayers from our church community.

Calling 911 and waiting for the professionals seems like what I'm supposed to do, but now I stand outside waiting, wondering if it will be enough. Why didn't I ditch my car and run down to the bridge?

I never imagined it would take so long for rescue workers to arrive. But roads around the region that were passable only an hour before are now closed. Lack of electricity adds to the traffic nightmare as signal lights are out around town. Rescuers are overrun with emergency calls from stranded motorists who have tried to drive on flooded roads.

I stand in my neighbor's front yard as the first police officer pulls up. He has me describe Jack's clothing. He asks if Jack could be pretending or hiding. I calmly answer his questions, trying to be as helpful as possible, but I wonder where his sense of urgency is. He moves slowly, seemingly in no hurry to go down to the creek. There is a child underwater right now! My child.

When the EMTs finally arrive, they spread out a map. "What's the name of this creek?"

None of us know. Does our crappy little neighborhood creek even merit a name?

I look at my neighbor Jenn, Alexis's mom, and mouth the words I can't say to rescue workers, "Someone needs to get in the fucking water!"

She nods, then holds me close. As we stand waiting, the EMTs speak of this being a five-hundred-year or one-thousand-year flood of epic proportions. I don't give a shit about how rare this flood is or that it is unlike anything we'd seen before or would ever see again in our lifetimes—I just want to find Jack.

But even in the chaos, I'm already becoming aware of the improbability of what is happening. A flood no one had known was coming. Lack of electricity on our side of town that hampered traffic and sent the kids out of their dark houses to play in the rain. Warm weather that made the afternoon feel like a blessed continuation of summer vacation. A fenced-in yard where for eight years my kids had never, ever played, so the fact that it led to a particularly hazardous section of the creek was completely off my radar. A neighborhood creek that was such a nonissue for us that we'd never once warned our kids about it. Parents and neighbors and children not heeding the thunder when it started so suddenly. A cautious child who was afraid of moving water getting too close to the edge of a creek and ending up in the water. How did all those things add up to *this*? It seems impossible. I don't understand.

As we stand in the neighbor's yard, I try to tell the rescuers to go out of the neighborhood, to the small bridge, because I feel in my heart that's where Jack is, yet I can't even remember the name of the road that we've lived off of for eight years to explain what I mean. I sigh and I point. I'll find out later that it is rescue policy to start searching where someone falls in, not where the water flows.

I hold Jenn's hand and kneel, cursing and praying in the grass of the neighbor's yard. The rain is now light. The thunder has passed. It is almost pleasant out. I look up at the people gathered around me—adults and children I know so well—and put my palms together. "Pray. Pray," I mouth to them, unable to speak aloud.

Kristen wraps a striped beach towel around my shoulders. It smells dank and wet. I feel terrible for noticing this small detail when Jack is trapped underwater somewhere. I'm not doing enough. I feel like I'm an actor in a bad movie and I'm botching my role. Should I pull off my soggy pants so I can run freely down through the woods? Should I scream and flail around? Why am I acting so calm? Am I a mother or a robot?

Tim pulls up and approaches me, stricken. He doesn't know what to do either. "Should I go down there?" he asks, confused.

"Yes. Go." How will he ever forgive me for this?

I don't go back down to the creek. I am quiet. The police tell me to go home and wait, "In case Jack shows up." Bullshit. But I do. I'm a Donaldson. We don't do drama. We rely on the experts. We like structure and order to keep the chaos at bay. And up to this point, we considered chaos to be our busy schedules and an active family life.

Jenn will walk Margaret home a few minutes later, to sit on my lap in the kitchen and then wait in her dark bedroom with friends until we know more. I don't run to the road, to the bridge, where they will find him, two hours later, trapped by enormous logs and debris in the murky darkness of a drainpipe. Where they root him out with a pole. His body has traveled five hundred yards. That's nearly the length of five football fields. I had known within seconds exactly where the raging waters had taken my boy. I don't know how, but I just knew. But I didn't go there. I didn't find him. I didn't save him.

I was close. So close, but close wasn't good enough.

seven

Istand in our darkened kitchen with my neighbors. I wonder, do you put something like this on Facebook to get people to pray, or is that tacky? Just an hour or so before, I'd posted: "Homework by Candlelight. Little House on the Prairie vibe—except for the documenting our every move on Facebook part."

Now, I stay off the Internet, but text a few friends these horrible words: "Jack swept away in creek. Presumed dead. Pray." What? He's been missing less than an hour and I'm writing "presumed dead" about a cautious, brown-eyed boy who is in perfect health, has never had a broken bone or stitches or even seen the inside of an emergency room. What's wrong with me? It's not as if anyone has told me he's not going to make it. Am I praying hard enough? Will praying even help, when I feel in my soul he is gone?

I don't remember calling my sister, Liz, who since our late teens has been my dearest friend. She lives five hours away and is at her son's football game. Later, she'll tell me she asked, "How long has he been in the water?" and I replied, "Too long." She immediately gets in her car and starts driving, calling our relatives on the way.

I text the mother of Margaret's best friend. She is confused, even though the same little creek winds through her own neighborhood. Water is such a nonissue in our town that even with the rainy day, she doesn't make any connection. She assumes from my text that Jack must be away with Tim on some Boy Scout trip. She texts back, "I don't understand. Who is Jack with?"

My reply: "Jesus." No one has told me anything yet, but I guess I just know.

Jesus.

I put out cheese and crackers for a friend with low blood sugar, knowing we have a long night ahead of us. A lone EMT stands outside our door, rain pooling on his rain gear. His assignment is to stay with "the mother" in case I have a medical incident. I don't know this then, of course, or that mothers in my position might scream or collapse or even quietly go off and harm themselves. I just know to stand, then sit, and wait for the news to come.

This EMT, who has seen heartbreak and tragedy more often than most over a twenty-year career, tells me later that he felt helpless that he couldn't take part in the rescue attempt as his coworkers tried desperately to find Jack. Instead, he keeps his post, waiting and watching me through the glass of the kitchen door. At one point he hears Margaret, who has curled up on my lap, wail, "But I don't want to be an only child!" and his heart, the heart of a father, feels like it is breaking into tiny pieces.

Tim comes up from the creek to wait, his one pair of work shoes covered in mud from trying to get close. From trying to do something. He tells me he knew if he tried to go into the water to save Jack that he would have surely died. He feels so helpless. The shoes will sit by the door in a plastic grocery bag for weeks, smelly and rank, while Tim, grieving and off-kilter, wears hiking boots to work.

At some point during these moments, we become "The Mother. The Father. The Sister." Are these our new identities? Will Jack, with his talents and gifts and a future so bright, be reduced to "The Boy in the Creek"?

In the next few hours, people come and go. Our pastor Linda shows up, as does the young pastor of a new church who is a friend of our neighbors. Neighbors who have thrown on rain gear and are walking through the woods, searching for any sign of Jack. As the young pastor pulls his car onto our street, he leans out the window, stopping someone on the sidewalk, where people have gathered. "Their names...what are their names?" he asks. "Tim and Anna." And so he will walk willingly into the house of pain, hoping that the God he believes in can somehow make this horrific situation better. He will have only our first names and his prayer book.

My dad and stepmother come, with candles and camping lanterns and umbrellas, and friends from school and church sit with Margaret in her darkened bedroom. The kids' principal and others try to make it, but more roads have closed by this point. The storm none of us had heard anything about, and had caught the entire Washington area by surprise, continues on.

Eventually the darkness outside matches the darkness in the house. And still we sit. Several police officers and a detective come in. Tim, the officers, the pastor, and I walk down to the family room for privacy, away from our friends in the kitchen. This is the room where our family snuggles on the leather couch watching movies, always lined up the same way in a row: Margaret, Tim, Anna, Jack. Where I stick my face in Jack's just-washed hair to inhale the scent of Old Spice. Where I wrap my arms around his bony shoulders and don't let go, no matter how long our show is, moving only to retuck toes when they spring free from our blanket. Where we had played Clue together just last night, after a great first day of school, and no one had gotten mad, and we had laughed and joked and even all made it to bed on time. Where the kids wrestle with the dog and dance around in their pj's and ooh and ahh over the Christmas tree each year. An enormous framed chalkboard over the fireplace reads: Donaldson Family, Established 1996. A small yellow canvas propped next to it adds "All things are possible," a nod to Jack's favorite Bible verse, "For nothing is impossible with God."

Nothing is impossible? What about what is happening to our family? The familiar room looks sinister and strange, its only light coming from police flashlights and candles. Inside my head I will the officers not to speak. *Don't say it. Don't you dare say it! You do not know us! You do not know our son! You do not know anything about this family!*

I do not want to hear what they are going to tell us, yet I am powerless to stop them. "We found Jack, but he didn't make it. We are sorry to say he is dead." Dead? Tim lets out a wail that comes from deep inside his body. It sounds primal and ancient, as if it has been lodged there for centuries.

I hold his heaving shoulders and then look back at the officers. They do not interview us or provide any information about what happened by the creek. They do not tell us where the kids had been playing or how Jack ended up in the water. I assume all that will come later, but I can barely think beyond this hellish moment. They tell us there will be an autopsy and that we can see his body the next day. That they are sorry he couldn't be saved. Autopsy? Body? What kind of freakish alternate universe is this? We cannot be talking about Jack. One officer hands his business card to Tim, and Tim takes it—such a normal motion, in such an abnormal circumstance.

I start speaking, looking directly at the three officers, "We are heartbroken by what you are telling us, but we're Christians. We don't grieve the way other people grieve, because we know our son is already in heaven." Huh? What am I saying? Was this a feeble attempt to convince myself that everything is going to be okay? Am I trying to impress the young pastor who stands near us, clutching his prayer book? Whose words are these? I look at the officers and wonder which one needs to hear what I am saying, because I feel as if I am addressing one of them specifically.

It's not the first time I've felt a prompting like this, and it won't be the last. I know it must be God's Spirit giving me the words to say. Even in that moment I am somehow aware that what is going on is more than the tragic story of just one family, so I let the Holy Spirit speak through me, for an unknown purpose. But truthfully, all I care about is Jack. Exactly seventy pounds of skin and bones and laughter and heart.

Tim and I hold each other, and I begin to sob, the officers and the pastor standing nearby. I can't quit wailing into his wet shoulder, "I am so, so sorry. I am so, so sorry!" How many times do I say it? Twenty? Thirty? It can never be enough, because I was the one who let the kids play in the rain. I was the one who had spent twelve years worrying and protecting and learning about every possible harm that could come to them from asbestos to lead paint to sexual predators to tick bites to bullying to porn. Yet it hadn't been enough! One of our babies is gone.

Tim's entire life has been relatively free of worry, pain, and despair, yet now he faces *this*? He seems so fragile in that moment. How can he possibly survive? How can we survive as a family? Are we even a family anymore? I am so, so sorry.

Tim tells me he thinks we should go to bed holding Margaret after we tell her the news, and I agree, so we send everyone home, except for a few friends who will wait in the kitchen until Liz arrives. The house is still so very dark. Tim and I climb the stairs together and sit on Margaret's twin bed in her newly painted aqua room. We have gone from being told the worst news imaginable to having to deliver this same message to a terrified, vulnerable ten-year-old. He and I hold hands, and we each put an arm around Margaret. I say, "Margaret, they found Jack, but he is dead. We are so sorry. We are going to take care of you, and everything is going to be okay." The words taste like bile in my mouth. How can I promise her anything when I couldn't keep Jack safe?

"No! No! No! No!" she sobs, gasping for breath. Eyes wide with fear, she shakes her head back and forth as if to expel this ludicrous thought from her brain. Tim picks her up, cradles her, and we walk down the hallway and the half flight of steps away from the children's bedrooms. How strange it seems to turn our backs on Jack's room at bedtime and just walk away. Folding ourselves around Margaret in our queen-size bed, the three of us cry.

Usually I'd start the bedtime routine in Margaret's room and spend a few minutes with her reading and then praying. We would hear Jack in the bathroom across the hall, brushing his teeth, thumping out the rhythm of some song on the countertop. "He's so loud!" Margaret would say when we finished our prayers. We would turn out her lamp, and she would almost be asleep by the time I pulled her ceiling fan cord, shut the door, and went into Jack's room for our snuggle time.

Jack always got me for the longest, because like me, he was a night owl. Tim would have finished doing a devotional or reading aloud from *The Lord of the Rings* with him when I came in. This was the bedtime dance, and after over a decade, we had it down pat.

But how can we pray now, in this situation, when the kids' bedrooms are empty? When Margaret's big brother, best friend, champion, and comforter will never climb into his twin bed again? Our nightly prayers always began, "Thank You, God, for this day." But we are *not* thankful for this day! We usually centered the prayers on people who were sick, or on our sponsor children on the other side of the world whom, I admit, I pitied because they did not have the resources and advantages Jack and Margaret had. Now they are alive and Jack is dead. We always ended with, "God bless Mom and Dad and Jack and Margaret and Shadow." None of this seems to fit tonight, but we hold on to each other and say the words anyway.

Margaret says something in the dark that dawns on her as a revelation. "All those times Jack and I said, 'This is the worst day ever!' it wasn't true. *This* is the worst day ever." She's right. After Margaret falls asleep, Tim and I reach across her body to hold hands and cry some more. I wonder how Tim will survive without Jack, the one he throws the baseball with each evening. The one who shares his humble nature and his handsome face. Will he see Jack when he looks in the mirror?

Together in the dark, we cannot know how or if we will survive. And we cannot know that it will be almost an entire year before we have this bed back to ourselves. In that moment it seems unfathomable to imagine separating the tiny, tattered remnant of our family, even for a moment, even in sleep. We need to be together.

The irony of the family bed is not lost on me. We of the structure, strict bedtime routines, and kids in their own rooms with doors closed. Of the exhausted sighs of relief when Tim and I would finally get grown-up time at night to watch TV. Of sinking into the couch together, but always muting the television within a few minutes when we'd hear Jack padding down the stairs to say to us, "I'm bored"—a quirky nighttime ritual that annoyed me mightily at first but then became something to look forward to, always ending with an extra hug and Jack traipsing back to his room.

Every single night I'd go through the entire bedtime routine, with kisses and good nights and serious conversation in the dark, knowing I'd see Jack just a few minutes later delivering his urgent message of "I'm bored. Did I tell you I'm bored?" Tonight, hoping to feel close to him, I whisper like a lunatic into the darkness, "I'm bored."

eight

I beg for sleep but will myself not to dream, for I am terrified of dreaming of the trauma Jack experienced in the creek. Of being trapped. Of struggling. Of being afraid. Of what his little body went through being dragged downstream, ripped out of his clothes, hitting fallen trees and rocks hidden under the raging water. Of dying without us there. Of drowning. Drowning? I can barely form that ugly word in my mind.

Before fitful sleep comes, I repeat over and over in my head, *Jack is dead. Jack is dead. Jack is dead.* These are the same words, the same rhythmic beat, that will run through my head as I drive down the street, windshield wipers swishing back and forth on yet another rainy Thursday, or push my cart through the grocery store trying to remember how to do some of the most mundane, basic tasks of mothering.

On this night I test these harsh and unfamiliar words, trying to convince myself of the impossible reality of what just happened. I don't want to fall asleep until I can believe it. I'm not sure what would be worse—dreaming about the horror of the accident or dreaming of Jack alive and whole and waking to realize he's not coming back.

I awake just a few minutes later to the sound of my sister sobbing in the guest room right next to Jack's room. She got here around midnight, with neighbors and friends waiting for her in the dark kitchen. Now I slowly walk up the stairs toward her, pausing at Margaret's empty room, the door wide open. Less than a month before, I had scrambled all week to surprise her with a room makeover before Tim and the kids returned from visiting his parents in Connecticut.

On the way into the house the day we'd revealed the room makeover to Margaret, Jack saw that a Lego set he had ordered weeks before had arrived in the mail. He held the box under his arm as we revealed Margaret's new room.

She looked at every detail, and he followed her around, slowly taking it all in—the paint, the furniture, the rug I'd made out of free carpet samples and duct tape. He touched the dresser, the lamp, the bookcase and mumbled words of approval. I remember thinking then, as I had so many times before, how Jack didn't make things be about himself. He was probably itching to open his package and get started on his own fun, but he stood next to Margaret, checking out every knob and special touch I'd made on her room, letting her have her moment, or maybe he was letting me have mine, but still being part of it too.

Liz has grown quiet, so instead of going to the guest room, I enter Jack's room and crawl into his bed, the texture of the surfboard sheets so familiar to me after years of snuggling there each night. This is where we had our discussions about friends, feelings, God, and sex. I remember one evening, Jack was determined, since he didn't get sex ed at his school, that he not miss out on any of the things the other kids learned. Under cover of the darkened room, I filled him in to make sure he wouldn't be left behind. "Tell me everything you know, Mom. Are you sure you don't know anything else?" I wonder if he could sense my smiles in the dark. I was so proud of my boy and grateful he could talk to me like this.

Our most interesting evening conversations usually occurred right after Boy Scout trips when a lot of new words were thrown around. Jack, like many other kids, realized that if you asked the juicy questions at bedtime, Mom would usually go for the bait and stay longer. I loved it. Then we would have our good-byes. That is, until he would come downstairs and tell us he was bored.

Now, lying in his bed, I yearn for Jack's scent, pressing my face deep into his pillow, reaching my arm over into his spot in the narrow bed where I would comfortably drape it around his middle. I imagine the vice grip he placed on my arm when I told him it was time for me to go. Sometimes the grip made me stay longer; other times I peeled his long fingers off one by one, eager to have time for myself. I would end our time together with, "I love you, Jack. I love the way God made you. I'm so glad that you're my son. Good night."

Bedtime is also when I would recite to him Jeremiah 29:11. "'For I know the plans I have for you,' declares the LORD, 'plans to prosper you and not to harm you, plans to give you hope and a future.'" I remember saying this to him one time, probably after a hard day, our faces so close I could feel a tear trickle down his cheek onto mine in the dark. Did Jack know something I didn't know? Did Jack doubt that God had a good plan for him? Did Jack know God's plan meant being ripped away from a family who loved him? Because Jeremiah 29:11, which we, like so many others, had used as some sort of blanket promise that life would be okay, sure seems like a load of bullshit to me now.

I can't smell Jack anyway, even burying my face in his pillow, and although I am in shock, I'm aware enough to remember that he had been stressed and restless the last few nights and had chosen to sleep in the guest-room bed where my sister is now lying. Can Liz smell him there?

Eventually I make my way downstairs again and sit on the living room couch, clutching Margaret's small pink Girl Scout flashlight. Maybe it's better I not sleep anymore, so afraid am I of seeing Jack trapped, battered, and bruised. We hadn't thought to ask to see him after he'd been found, and now his body is in some strange place, naked, cold, and alone.

I check message after message on my phone as friends stay up all night weeping and praying. I will later learn details about how and when each found out about Jack. How they vomited, sobbed, railed at God, and hugged their kids with a scary fierceness. How they reasoned it couldn't be our Jack because he was so cautious. How they held out hope at first when the police released the wrong name to the press and said the creek was in "the victim's" backyard. They knew we didn't have a creek behind our house.

Eventually our friends find out the truth and must steel themselves to tell their children that Jack is dead. I don't know any of this that night; I just try to breathe and take some comfort knowing there are people awake with me. Facebook had been a fun way to reconnect with friends from different stages of my life. Now it becomes vital to try to stave off the loneliness and isolation that threaten my survival.

In the beam of my tiny flashlight, I see something that makes me gasp and then laugh out loud. I wonder if Tim or Liz hear me and will come downstairs to find out what's going on. On the wall in front of me, I see a huge silhouette of a head, about three feet wide and four feet tall. It is indisputably Jack. The cheeks, the cute nose—nothing like mine—the shape of his head, the distinctive way his hair effortlessly spikes up in front in what we call his "floop." I've always loved silhouettes, so much so that I'd had my friend Theresa make pillows for this room with Jack's and Margaret's silhouettes on them. And now Jack's silhouette looms large on the wall in front of me, as if projected on a screen. How I love that face.

Something strange is happening, as it had when the police told us Jack was dead. It does not give me comfort, because only having Jack back in his twin bed upstairs, in his butter-soft sheets, surrounded by Legos and doodles and good books, could do that. But it does make me feel again, instantly, that something spiritual is going on, and that as bereft and lonely as I feel, I am not alone.

I hold the flashlight in the same position for as long as I can, not wanting to lose the image, wanting to share it with someone. Tim staggers downstairs awhile later, and I show him my "magic flashlight." We sit on the couch and cry together again. I don't remember if we speak. I grab a tissue from the box in front of me. And then the image changes. My "magic flashlight" was really just a beam of light shining on the tissue box. The tissue sticking out had cast an image on the wall that looked exactly like Jack's profile. And now that I've used the tissue, the shadow I'm left with looks more like Bart Simpson or maybe even a rooster than Jack Donaldson. This makes me laugh again at the absurdity of it all.

The power finally comes on around 2 a.m. Tim takes my cell phone and his to charge in the kitchen. Stupid phones. Again, I lament not buying Jack a phone. I had reasoned that he was always either with me, at Clark and Donna's house, or in the cul-de-sac. He had never left our tiny neighborhood without us, which was a far cry from the way I was raised in the seventies and eighties, making daily trips to 7-Eleven for candy and Cokes, hanging out by myself in the woods, at the pool, or just exploring. The kids were growing up so fast, and I just thought there would be plenty of time later for phones and freedom and teenage things.

If he'd had a phone, I could be scrolling through texts from him, simple words from him to me, proving that he, we, mother and child, Jack and Mom, had really existed. But I don't have texts. What if I lose all memory of him just as I've lost him? We say, "So-and-So lost a child," but, my God, I really did LOSE him. He was right there on the edge of the creek, and then he wasn't. Unbelievable.

The sole voice mail I have on my cell phone from Jack is eerily prescient. Earlier in the summer I said he could play at two houses on our cul-de-sac, but that if the kids changed houses, he had to borrow a phone and let me know. Instead of his usual, rushed, mumbling speech, Jack says clearly, in a formal yet singsong way, "Hello? This is Jack. *Your son.* I am leaving Joe's house and going back to Daniel's house. So if you look at Joe's house, well, you sure won't find me there! Good-bye!"

You're right about that, Jack. We looked at Joe's house and didn't find you there. And now I want to die.

As soon as Tim plugs my phone into the charger, an image pops up. Not my usual password screen or the bar to slide. Instead, a Bible verse appears and fills the screen: Romans 8:38–39 (ESV).

> For I am sure that neither death nor life, nor angels nor rulers, nor
> things present nor things to come, nor powers, nor height nor depth,
> nor anything else in all creation, will be able to separate us from the
> love of God in Christ Jesus our Lord.

Tim had put this Bible app on my phone for Jack to use. Although Jack was an outstanding student who did his homework without prodding, Bible memory time was fraught with tension. He would want to recite his verses to me, and no matter what I did, it wasn't quite right. Maybe I would nod too much, clear my throat at an inopportune moment, correct him too much or too little. Perhaps it was my facial expressions that rankled him.

By the time we were finished with the assignment, Jack would have his verses memorized, but we would be pissed at each other, mad at his teacher for assigning such long verses, and even annoyed at the writers of the Bible for using confusing language. I told Jack I refused to work with him on his verses anymore because all it did was irritate me and it certainly wasn't doing much to instill a love of God's Word in either of us.

Tim put two Bible applications on my phone so Jack could test himself and leave me out of it. Now, almost four months since Jack had last used that application, this beautiful and comforting verse pops up, just hours after Jack suffered a violent death in the creek. Nothing could separate us from the "love of God in Christ Jesus our Lord." Nothing? Not even this? I have to believe it.

The silhouette on the wall and the verse on the phone are two of the first signs we have that God is right here with us in the pain. *He'd better be,* I think. *Because I am not going to make it otherwise.*

nine

In the later morning I again say to myself, "Jack is dead. Jack is dead," just in case any magical thinking has taken hold of me. I want to make sure I haven't tried to change things in my mind, maybe getting to the creek just a moment sooner or never even moving to this neighborhood in the first place.

Why did I want a bigger house? Why did a family with kids move into the house by the creek? Why hadn't *we* bought a house with a creek in the backyard, so at least I could have warned the kids about the power of the water over the years? Why hadn't the electric company trimmed the branches that sat on our power lines? What if I had just said, "Stay inside"? What if Tim had come home early with a pizza? What if I hadn't given up so soon? On this morning, I'm tempted to try to rewrite the story, altering just one tiny part of it, making myself more attentive, more virtuous, or braver, so we'll end up with different results.

The maddening thing is that even with a storm of epic proportions, even with letting the kids play outside in the rain, even with a swollen creek, the story could have ended up differently, as it did for hundreds of other children in our region. I'll hear from their mothers in letters and e-mails over the next weeks, as they generously assure me that I was not alone in letting my kids play outside on that strangely wonderful, horrible day. Writing to me is a duty they carry because their kids came home. Their evenings ended with wet, happy children peeling off T-shirts and shorts and settling in for dinner and showers and bedtime.

Maybe I can insert a locked gate into Jack's story. Joe's mom leaning out her rear window saying, "Don't go down there!" Maybe I can send a text to Jack on his nonexistent cell phone saying, "Come home."

But I know that all my scheming and thinking won't amount to crap, so to ensure I'm operating in reality, I once again repeat the awful truth that has not yet settled into my heart or my brain, "Jack is dead. Jack is dead." It's like I'm speaking a strange language, trying to figure out how to shape my mouth around the bizarre words.

When Jack and Margaret had speech therapy as preschoolers, they'd screw their mouths into funny shapes and repeat their practice words so many times: "wool, wool, wooooool," that the words ceased to seem real. So maybe saying "Jack is dead" won't be much help after all. My mind is a jumble of shock, sadness, and disbelief. And a longing for Jack so severe that I tell myself that even five more minutes with him would be enough. Please just give me five more minutes! I want to hold him. I want to kiss him. I want to say good-bye.

And all this plotting and begging could be turned around in an instant by Jack coming down to the kitchen for breakfast. I could stick my face in his hair and inhale, knowing that it's all been a bizarre dream. I could relax, hand him a box of cereal, and go back to an innocent place of blessed unknowing. I always thought that denial was a refusal to accept the truth. I'm *trying* to believe that Jack is dead. I am. I guess on some level I know it must be true because he's not here with us, but I'm bewildered at how it could have happened at all. Is that denial? Maybe *disbelief* is a better word.

It's even more confusing because Jack was not a rough-and-tumble kind of guy, and when people described someone as "all boy," they certainly weren't talking about him. Jack was as comfortable playing word games, drawing, and doing puzzles as he was bouncing on a trampoline or running around. When I worried about him, it was that someone would do something to harm him or he would become ill, not once that he would be in an accident.

As a toddler, he would walk to the very end of our driveway and his toes would not cross an imaginary line there. When friends found out Tim and I weren't spankers, they'd test me, "Yeah, but what if Jack ran into the street or pulled away from you in a parking lot or a store? Wouldn't you spank him then?"

"Uh, well, I'm not thinking that's going to happen" was my reply. And it never did. Perhaps I was naive, but he was just so cautious.

Jack didn't make a big deal about holding back from risky ventures; he just quietly declined. He didn't like roller coasters or the ocean's waves. He was the only kid who never went off the rope swing from the riverbank on our camping trips. Even his little sister tried it. He didn't ride his bike outside the neighborhood. Or go on the paddleboats in Washington, DC. Or skateboard. Or ride dirt bikes. He had me talk to the director of his summer camp in July to make sure his group was not going white-water rafting or on any high-adventure activities he wasn't comfortable with. "I think that might give me 'the stomach feeling,' Mom," he explained.

Jack ran home immediately to tell me when some neighbors played with matches, and he didn't act embarrassed of me when I'd call kids out for dangerous behavior. Even at twelve, he never jockeyed to sit in the front seat of the car, knowing he didn't yet meet the size requirements. Sure, Jack did love being outside and the increasing freedom that came with growing older. He loved to hike, go caving, and climb trees. Skiing with Tim was one of his favorite activities. He loved baseball and tolerated soccer and football. So Jack wasn't a couch potato, but he was not a big risk taker either.

It's so hard to grasp. Even a month from now, back in southern Virginia, Liz will call, failing to hold back the tears that always seem so close to the surface these days, pain and disbelief in her voice. "I don't get it. If there was a poster child for 'kid least likely to get swept away in a stupid creek,' Jack would be the one." Amen, sister. Jack's classmate Christy will tell me later she sometimes pretends he's just in the bathroom during school. I get it. Frankly, that makes more sense to me than Jack drowning.

My shattered mind won't even begin wanting details about those final moments for months to come. And by then, it will be difficult to piece together what happened by the creek. Were the kids horsing around? Making dares? Where were they standing when Jack lost his footing or, if for some unimaginable reason, he stepped off the edge? Did he cry out? Was he afraid, or was the last look on his face one of laughter and joy?

It won't be until six months after the accident that I will call on the officer who wrote and signed the police report. She will come over, and I will tell her that Tim and I are finally ready to hear details of that night. Terrifying as it is to have a uniformed officer in our house again, I'll do it because I think it's an important part of grieving. I figure there will be loads of information I've avoided: photos of where the kids were standing, estimates of how deep the water was, interviews, a time line. But after the officer reads a few scant sentences, which incorrectly report that Jack was playing with only one other child that night and make no mention of my ever coming down to the creek, I'll realize she is finished. I ask her in a breaking voice why that's all there is.

She answers me, "Our job wasn't to try to find out what happened; it was to make sure no one else got hurt." Tim and I sit numbed and silenced by the shock of her words. Wasn't Jack worth more than this?

I will wonder if the other families involved in the accident had wished their children were interviewed extensively that night or in the first few days when things were still fresh. That's how I'll feel about Margaret, who was never interviewed, that somehow in the retelling of her story to the police, the grip it now has on her would have been released.

After our fruitless meeting with the officer, I realize that never knowing exactly what Jack's final seconds were like will be another loss for Tim and me, one that we couldn't have fathomed on this first horrible day.

So here I am the day after the accident, in the corner of my couch, finding it so hard to grasp that out of all the kids who played outside in our region yesterday, Jack is the one who is gone. That he is a news event. That he isn't coming home.

I keep saying in my mind: *Jack? JACK? Really?*

But maybe all deaths feel like this—improbable, strange, untimely, unnatural. Maybe every single death needs to be examined, spoken of aloud, and turned over in the mind to make it seem more real. And perhaps not being able to grasp all at once what has happened is a small mercy in itself. Maybe the "Jack is dead" part of our brains is in a deep freeze and needs to thaw bit by bit, with one painful realization after the other instead of all at once, so as not to kill us too.

News of Jack's death spreads that Friday. All schools are closed due to flooding, something I've never experienced as a student, teacher, or parent living here for more than forty years. We are not a town on water. There are a few small ponds in subdivisions and paltry creeks that run through wooded neighborhoods and across the golf course, havens for tadpoles and mosquitoes. Schools hadn't opened late or closed early yesterday due to weather, and I'd noticed no information about the potential for flash floods in the *Washington Post* or on the radio as I drove the kids to school. Nothing. Now I learn just how crazy it had been, with people waiting hours to get home, daredevils tubing down Route 50, a four-lane road, and four deaths in our region. Jack is the only child to die.

As new seventh graders wake up to a surprise holiday on this beautifully sunny day, moms with swollen eyes walk into their bedrooms to break the news. Jack's classmates, their moms, and the school principal soon gather at a home to pray, laugh, and cry. When I hear that, my first thought is, *Jack would love getting together with his friends on a free day!* Oh.

Someone erects a cross near the road outside our neighborhood where Jack's body was found. Neighbors take on the task of arranging food and trying to keep news cameras away. We feel vulnerable and exposed with our uncovered kitchen window facing the driveway—a tableau of grief and misery—but we never had a need for curtains until now. Friends quickly cover the glass with butcher paper and tape.

I sit like a zombie in the corner of our couch, hugging people when they come to comfort us. Aunt Betty's here. My brother, John. My friend Cindy from church is going to scan pictures of Jack for us. I guess that's what you do. She leans to hug me, then stands to hug Tim.

"Don't ever leave us," he chokes into her shoulder.

"I won't."

As if any of us can make promises anymore.

Suzie, my friend since college, helps us write a statement for the press that will give them information but will also help us maintain some privacy:

> Last night, we lost our beloved son and brother, Jack. Words cannot describe our grief and sadness. Jack was an extraordinary, faith-filled, clever and witty child who loved his family and God above all else. Jack enjoyed Legos, acting, and baseball. Jack loved making others laugh and sharing in their happiness. He will be forever missed. We thank the community for their prayers and support.

Daniel and his cousin Lily are interviewed by a reporter in the cul-de-sac. More reporters leave messages on our machine and pass along business cards through our neighbors, who have closed off the driveway with little kiddie traffic cones to try to protect us. We don't dare watch the news, so fearful are we of seeing frightening images to be etched in our minds forever. Did people see his body being found and taken away?

Someone brings us our mail. There's a Hot Wheels car Jack ordered last week, a special one he'd been looking for. "Give it to Daniel," I tell Tim. "That's what Jack would have wanted." How many times will we say those words in our new, horrible lives? How will Daniel, only ten years old, endure looking out of his grandparents' window every single day into our house with no Jack?

"Do you think you could try just a bite or two?" my stepmother asks as morning turns to afternoon. I look down at the paper plate of chicken salad, nod, but make no move to lift the fork. My hand feels heavy, as if the trip from plate to mouth would be an unnaturally long one. The thought of any food, or even water, makes my stomach turn.

I'm still sitting in the corner of the couch. Relatives arrive and depart. Some stand in our sunny driveway and talk in quiet voices. They brainstorm ways to help, to fill needs we don't even know we have yet. Tim has told Margaret that we will ask for donations in Jack's memory, so she's been on the computer, searching for charities that have to do with either Legos or lobsters, two things that remind her of Jack. This is the first day of life she's ever lived without him.

Friends take her to the craft store as a diversion while people come and go from the house. They make T-shirts, some with Jack's name emblazoned on them with glittery iron-on letters and angel wings. Margaret's shirt is the least flashy of the bunch, and already it registers with me that her grief will be more private, less showy, as she tries to find any sense of normalcy in an abnormal situation. I wonder if the sun seems unnaturally bright to Margaret today as it does to me. Does she feel vulnerable leaving our house, even in the safe confines of a friend's familiar minivan? Does the world seem different, foreign, and frightening now?

My friend Rebecca unfurls a red tablecloth for an extra table. Where did that come from? I become aware that the community is bringing up food, serving dishes, utensils, and paper products from their own houses so as not to burden us in any way by digging through our drawers and cabinets or asking where things are. The dishes will disappear as quickly as they have come, whisked away by efficient helpful hands. Our friends expect no acknowledgment of their efforts, just the chance to do something, anything, to try to make an impossible situation just a little better. They greet me with hugs and gentle smiles, but I see the horror in every set of eyes.

I know I should keep track of who is doing what. But I just can't, so I sit. A neighbor with four little ones will drive up our driveway each day to replenish ice in the jumbo cooler—whose cooler?—that sits filled with sodas in the carport.

I reach my hand out to touch the antique hutch next to me. This is where I keep my tablecloths. They're right here. They're white. I barely use them because I hate to iron. They're folded up next to the colorful flags we hang on the front stoop throughout the year. Easter, Valentine's Day, Christmas, birthdays. The Snoopy one that says Live, Love, Laugh. I want to pitch in, to say, "I am a mom with tablecloths and holiday flags. I am one of you. I have a grocery list right inside that cupboard door. Most of my plastic containers have matching lids."

But I can't enter into the planning and the serving and the helping and the doing because I am *The Mother*. I can't be privy to the phone calls and e-mails: "Did you hear?" "Oh God. No!" "What are they going to do?" "How will they survive?" "How can we help?" Those conversations are for the community, for the helpers, of whom there are many.

On their own they will find ways to memorialize Jack and show us love. They will sit around kitchen tables making small crosses out of Legos for everyone to wear at the memorial service on Monday. They will cook. They will write blog posts. They will tie royal-blue ribbons of remembrance on mailboxes, trees, lampposts, and Stop signs all over town, so we'll see them as we drive, Jack's seat gapingly empty next to Margaret.

Later, when they begin to question God and try to make sense of the panicked insecurity they now feel for the future, for the safety of their own children, they won't be able to share that with me either. They won't want to burden me with their own doubts, pain, therapist visits, and fitful sleep when I am reeling from the greatest pain any of us could have ever imagined. If we had even let ourselves imagine it.

I reach out to touch the drawer full of unused tablecloths. I want to be part of the doing, the fixing, the processing, but I can't. My role here is different. Instead, I sit, receive, and cling to the ridiculous belief inside, the tiny flicker, really, that in some inexplicable way, this is all going to be okay. I remember feeling that flicker after my mom died. The tiny hope to go on. But this is my child, this is new territory, so all bets are off.

ten

Less than twenty-four hours after I let the kids go out and play, we must go to the funeral home, the only one in our town. I can't stand that place. I feel rushed, and I want to resist. I want to sit down on the kitchen floor like an angry toddler, or turn my legs limp like spaghetti, so no one can make me do this!

Just three weeks ago I was at the same funeral home for my friend's father's funeral, pushing through painful memories of losing my mother that welled up inside me. I chose to help set up the house for a reception after the service instead of going to the graveside. I told another friend, "I don't do cemeteries if I can help it." How flip I was. Don't *"DO cemeteries"*? I don't have much of a choice now, do I?

As we leave the house, Tim and I see an enormous tan bird circling and swooping slowly over the house in graceful arcs against the brilliant sky. It is huge, so large that it strikes me as almost prehistoric. Could a hawk be this big? I have the fleeting thought that a pterodactyl could land on our front lawn today and that wouldn't seem as crazy to me as what is happening to our family.

My brother and sister put Tim and me in my brother's truck and drive us less than a mile to the funeral home. It is on our major road. The same road where Jack's body was discovered. If I make a left out of our neighborhood, I drive over the spot where his body was trapped in the drainpipe. If I make a right? The funeral home. These are the only ways out.

How will I do it? How will I do this every day? I haven't yet considered that just looking out my kitchen window I will see a group of healthy children play-ing without Jack, yet playing the games he made up for them. That I will be jealous that all these other kids are alive and Jack is dead. That every time I drive up my street I'll have to pass the house where the accident happened. That to take Margaret to school, I'll have to drive over the creek and back again. Those realizations will dawn later, painful as a knife stab and unrelenting, as I have to face them again and again and again. People talk about the different rungs of hell. Is this what they mean? Each realization dawning more horrible than the one before?

My brother, John, stays in the truck. Liz, Tim, and I pad up the stairs to a room in the funeral home, and all I can think of is that Jack's body is here somewhere. I try not to visualize where his body spent last night, away from us. I think of how overprotective a few neighbors thought I was when I'd sit on our metal glider, overseeing the kids playing in the driveway. When I would rarely let them have sleepovers. When I monitored what they could watch on TV or access on the computer. It was simply not worth the risk to me. None of it was. But now their kids are all fine, and my son has spent the night in a refrigerator somewhere.

We sit in florid Victorian-looking chairs and listen to what the woman is saying to us. Tim and I hold hands. How are we supposed to make decisions about memorializing Jack when our brains can't even grasp what happened just hours before? Mere hours since I let the kids go out and play, and now we need to decide about cremation versus burial and figure out what to write in an obituary.

I think of our "Summer To-Do List" still hanging on the fridge, even though summer is now over. Each year we would write down what we wanted to do as a family. "Go to the top of the Washington Monument." Check. We got that one in right before the strange August earthquake closed it down indefinitely. "Spend the night in a motel." Check. "See *Transformers* movie." Check. Nothing huge or fancy here, just a family's simple list to try to make the most of our time together.

The last two items remain undone. "Have people over." That one was Jack's. He loved to bring people together. And now our house is full of family and friends who love us, but does it really count when Jack isn't there? The last item, added by Margaret and me, was incomplete because Jack thought it was far too risky: "White-Water Rafting."

We are shocked. Shocked. It's really the only way to describe the way we feel. Jack was spinning in the driveway in the rain. Now he's gone? We are in a funeral home? Preposterous.

Jack is not at a friend's house. He's not at camp. He's not at school. He is dead. I move my head slowly, side to side, and squint as if trying to shake off a blurry haze that has descended on me. I'm trying to clear the crazy out of my mind and get back to what is rational and real.

We find out that dying so close to a weekend and having a memorial service on a Monday—when did we decide that?—puts things on a real rush course. We quickly write an obituary before the weekend newspaper deadline. No one mentions including a photo. When we get home I will worry about this, wishing the whole region could see Jack's young face staring out among the old dead people in the obituary section of the *Washington Post*. Instead, there will be an article on the front page and a photo inside. Good. This is all so wrong, and I want people to see it. We sign the death certificate.

The woman asks if we want to see Jack. I feel sick. I wonder if we are terrible parents that we didn't insist on seeing him last night by the side of the road. Holding him in his naked, wet brokenness. Had that been an option? It didn't even occur to us as we sat obediently in our dark house. And now we aren't even sure if we want to see him. The prospect seems terrifying, and we must decide right now.

Liz bravely says she'll go in first and let us know what she thinks. She is not a dispassionate observer. She is Auntie. She cut the umbilical cord when Tim, tears in his eyes, saw the flash of scissors and held back, afraid of somehow hurting tiny, newborn Jack. She is his biggest supporter. She had seen her "Jackie-Boy" come into the world, and now she would be a brave witness to what his body looked like when he left it.

Liz comes back, wobbly but resolute. What was it like for her alone in the room with him? "He has some injuries, but I think you should do it," she says. She thinks it will help us really grasp that Jack is dead.

I understand. I stood by my mother's side as she breathed her last, raspy breath, but Liz and our brother, John, never had the chance to see her body. There was no viewing, plus a closed casket at her funeral. We found out later that my grandparents had asked to go into the church a few minutes early to open the casket and see her before she was buried. They needed some way to understand that their vibrant daughter was dead at only forty-six.

I know that seeing a body can be important. But *Jack's* body? Oh, my beautiful boy. I just don't know if I can do it. His hands! Will I see his distinctive, creative hands with their long, knobby fingers? The hands that built with Legos and doodled and painted? What condition is he in? And what about Margaret? Should we have brought her with us? We'll find out later she has convinced herself Jack was abducted by a stranger, which seems far more plausible to her young mind than his getting too close to the edge of a creek and being swept away. But what if seeing his body horrifies and haunts her? Hasn't she been through enough? I need time to think! But there is none.

Tim and I enter the small room. Jack is on a table, covered up to his neck by a sheet. His two-day-old haircut is perfect. His beautiful face is scraped and battered but is still Jack, with those full lips and unbelievably long eyelashes. I know I am supposed to touch him. To hug him. To hold his skinny hand as I've done every day of his life, to brush my lips again across his velvety soft cheek. This can be an important part of the process. But my mind is a jagged jumble.

What's going on under that sheet? What if it's pulled up so far to cover something too ghastly to consider? Is his body intact? Who has broken my little boy? What the hell is happening? I hear a scream erupting from deep inside me. Tim is moaning something I don't understand. I reach out to touch Jack but can only force myself to pat my fingers one time against his beautiful hair, an awkward, fumbling touch, not the loving touch of a mother. His hair is cold, so cold. I stagger to the door, a side door I pass every single day on my drives around town, and it dumps me out in the sunlight onto the sidewalk beside the road. I don't know if Tim will follow or where my brother and sister are.

I look up and see a news reporter, stationed at the gyro shop across the street, perfectly groomed and speaking to the camera. It takes a second for me to register what she's doing there: Jack. Kids don't die in Vienna every day. Jack is news. I feel like I am prey, weakened and wounded, an easy target to be stalked and trapped. I pull Jack's green hoodie more tightly around me and feel myself shrinking as I sink down to the curb, out of the camera's sight.

It's official. Jack is dead. I want to die too. Back in the truck, I can't seem to stop yelling in an unfamiliar voice, "That was a mistake! That was a mistake!" I mean seeing the body, but so much more. There is nothing right about my son being dead, battered, naked, and alone. It all must be a mistake. Tim and I keen and wail all the way home.

eleven

Monday morning, three-and-a-half days after the accident, we pull into the gravel driveway of the small cemetery. Weathered headstones going back to Civil War times tilt at odd angles. Sparse grass is starting to grow over the newer plots, the dirt still peeking through. About thirty family members step out of cars into the bright sunshine. We walk over the uneven ground to stand next to my mother's gravestone, stained with age.

I've been here only a dozen times over the years, mostly in my teens and twenties, usually at dusk. Tim wanted us to bring the kids here regularly, but I never really connected the cemetery with my mom, so instead I told the kids stories of her driving me to middle school in her bathrobe, whistling as she arranged flowers, crying while singing "How Great Thou Art," and doodling on the back of any scrap of paper she could find.

We've planned Jack's burial to be private and held before the funeral service so the media won't find out about it. There will be no hearse. No funeral procession. It's not that I don't want people to know and care about Jack, or to have his short life be worthy enough to snarl traffic in our little town, but I don't want us to be on TV burying our son. It seems too raw and intimate for public consumption. We are burying him right next to my mom, the "Grandma Margaret" whom he'd never met.

I wear a gray dress I picked up for thirty bucks last year. It's my go-to dress, and I'd worn it in our family Christmas photo, the last one that would have all of us in it. In the haze of shock and pain, I forget that if I wear this dress today, I'll never be able to force myself to put it on again. Liz makes the smart move and borrows an outfit from my neighbor.

Last year Jack told Margaret and me he didn't like the idea of cremation. I smiled and chalked it up to one of his many firm but quirky preferences that came out in our conversations. Like how he was thoroughly troubled by the concept of a sperm bank. When I explained to the kids that my friend was doing IVF to have a baby, Jack looked at me in horror and said, "She didn't have to go to a *SPERM BANK,* did she?" perhaps picturing a stately brick building with tellers, deposit slips, a vault, and lots of little vials behind a counter.

"No, they used her husband's, uh, sperm," I answered. Were we really having this conversation? Regarding cremation, I pressed him a little because I wanted to be cremated someday and I knew Jack and Margaret would likely be the ones making those arrangements. "What's so bad about cremation?" I asked.

"Well, what if you're not really dead? At least in a coffin, you can yell and someone will let you out," he said. Dear God, please tell me someone checks those things. Please.

We had to make a rushed decision on burial versus cremation. I knew Jack's feelings on the matter, and I wept with pain at the thought of going against them. Margaret even reminded me of Jack's views right before Tim and I left for the funeral home. I said, "I know, honey, but I may need to decide this for me, not for Jack." I didn't explain how hard it had been for me over the years to imagine my mother's body under the ground through the cold winters and hot summers. I didn't tell Margaret how the thought used to keep me up at night and frighten me, and that I couldn't possibly endure that with Jack.

"We really need to know now what your decision is. It's almost the weekend," the funeral director pressed us. Tim and I walked into the room full of coffins. My father and stepmother had offered to pay for whatever we needed, taking the stinging injustice of having to pay for our boy's funeral off the long list of horrors we faced. Coffins lined the room. Open, closed, shiny metal, gleaming wood. Some cost more than our cars.

"Fucking waste," I said, about the cost of a coffin and a little boy's life cut short. Nothing about my lively boy belonged here. I felt my hands go clammy, and my mouth was dry as if I'd throw up any second. I knew, for me, there could be no coffin for Jack. No one would put makeup on his face covering whatever injuries were there and prop him on silky pastel cushions as if he were just sleeping. Because he wasn't.

In the cemetery two women from the funeral home stand holding a wooden box next to a small hole in the ground, a mound of ugly orange dirt piled next to it. I know then that we'd made the best worst decision possible by choosing to have Jack cremated. I was afraid that seeing a coffin might have killed me, knocked me to the ground and left me there, or had me throwing myself into the hole along with him. Maybe that sounds pretty dramatic and improbable for a person like me, but this whole situation was so unfathomable, could the past really serve as a reliable reference point?

I didn't want a coffin, but I don't want this little box either. I know once the women standing in the grass hand it to us this will all be real. Jack will be dead. He won't throw open the kitchen door, kick off his shoes, pull his black wooden stool up next to Margaret's at the counter, and wonder where we all are. The box negates that possibility.

It won't be until later that I'll think of the Bible verse that God gave Margaret in July and will realize it spoke of both water and fire, just like the past three and a half days of our lives. "When you pass through the waters, I will be with you; and when you pass through the rivers, they will not sweep over you. When you walk through the fire, you will not be burned; the flames will not set you ablaze."

Water? Flames? Were those words given to Margaret because she'd be spared these things while her brother would not? Or were they for Jack, whose body would endure them, but whose soul would never be overwhelmed or consumed because he was with God? I don't know.

Standing in this little cemetery on this gorgeous September day, I feel like I've been forced onto a scary, dangerous amusement-park ride, constructed by a psychopath, not a loving God. I'm strapped and buckled in, and the ride will move forward despite anything I might do to try to stop it. It will terrify me, make me sick, and possibly kill me, but there's no slowing it down once it starts. There can be no bargaining about taking this ride tomorrow or the next day instead. And there's no getting off.

Seeing the small wooden box, with an inlaid cross on the side, helps my shattered brain begin to know that Jack is gone, even though I'll have to re-realize it every day for months before it can sink in. I know that my Jack wouldn't fit in that shitty little overpriced box. I look down at Margaret in her sweet navy-and-white-striped dress, bare legs, and flip-flops. What is she thinking? Can a barely ten-year-old brain compute what mine struggles to understand?

After a few words and prayers by our pastors, Tim, Margaret, and I lean over and each drop a tiny Lego brick into the hole. So well trained are we by Jack to prize each plastic brick as a treasure, we feel a little wasteful committing them to the earth. Red, green, then blue. Maybe we should have chosen red, yellow, and blue because that's one of our family's sayings. One person calls out, "Red, yellow, blue...," and the other responds, "I love you!" But green is Jack's favorite color, chartreuse, really, and our brains are addled, so I'm relieved we've thought to do anything at all. Tim kneels down and gently places the box in the ground, then the three of us stand to the side, holding hands as our extended family looks on. It's the first time I'll consider the words "the three of us" rather than "the four of us." It sounds wrong. We are calm and composed. And we walk back to the cars.

We go home for lunch provided by our neighbors, and then it's time to leave for the funeral. I desperately want to slow things down. I feel there are details left undone, such as the obituary picture, hiring a limo to get us to the church, or scheduling visiting hours, but it's too late now. I call it a funeral, but I guess it's technically a memorial service or celebration of life because there won't be a body in the church. I don't know. Is *celebration of life* a bogus term anyway? Can we really celebrate a life cut short at twelve years old? He wouldn't even turn twelve and a half until next week.

I don't think of explaining to Margaret what goes on at a funeral, even though she's never attended one before. Plenty of characters die in kids' movies, usually an unfortunate mother, before the opening credits have even rolled, but I don't think they portray funerals very often. I should have prepped her.

I should have been informative and direct, the way I am when talking to the kids about sex. "We'll sing a few hymns, and then the pastors will say nice things about Jack. There will be no body or coffin there; Jack's ashes are in the little box we put in the ground. When we walk in and out, everyone will look at us, which might make you feel embarrassed. Afterward, Dad and I will be busy talking to people, but you can hang out in my office or outside with your friends if it seems like too much." I don't think of having that conversation until later. Grief books have helpful suggestions about what to say to small children, and they even encourage letting siblings see the body, but those books aren't really the sort of thing you know to read in advance.

I'm relieved to have forgotten about a limo. I know my bright, spunky girl will ride in one someday, for a prom or her wedding or even a lucky girl's birthday party, and I'm glad her special moments won't be clouded by the flashbacks of riding to her brother's funeral. I frantically try to print out the words I'll read at the service, but my printer coughs and jams. Grabbing a flash drive, I'm ready to go. No, not really ready, but resolved.

Tim, Margaret, and I climb back into John's pickup truck and make the five-minute drive to church. The parking lot is full, but someone waves us into a space saved for us with an orange traffic cone. This gesture makes me want to cry with gratitude for the acts, big and small, being done for us, many of which we'll never fully know. We will never be able to thank the thousands of people putting kindness out into the world in response to Jack's death. News cameras set up just off church property don't seem to notice us, which is a relief. Maybe they're looking for a limo.

As we enter the foyer filled with people who love us, we look down, avoiding eye contact as we head to the church parlor to wait. I feel the love surrounding us, but it is also the first time I feel diminished and utterly separate from the world. Separated by the fact that we'd "lost Jack," literally and figuratively, and as much as we are loved and cherished, it is our loss to bear.

No one has ever told me grief feels a lot like shame.

twelve

Octuber 1999, I placed baby Jack on the changing table, holding his soft tummy with one hand and flipping the origami cranes on his mobile with the other. The colorful paper birds swirled, Jack giggled, and I said, "Bird," as I always did. His huge brown eyes moved back and forth as I grabbed a diaper from the shelf below and put it on his wiggly body, his feet kicking with baby delight.

Then, thrusting his hand in the air, he made a waving motion, just as I had when I set the mobile in motion. It was his sign for bird. "Bird," he said. "Biiiird." This seven-month-old baby, who babbled and cooed and contorted his cute mouth this way and that trying to form words, yet came off more like a meowing kitten most of the time, had said his first word as clear as day!

After snapping his onesie, I planted a noisy kiss on the fat, delicious folds of his neck, scooped him up, and went to find our bulky video camera, hoping to get a reenactment on film. Jack and I spent long, long hours together while Tim worked and went to law school each night. I wasn't about to let this moment go undocumented. One, because it was simply the cutest, most magnificent thing I'd ever seen. Two, I didn't want it to look like all those hours cooped up in the house with a baby were making me hear things. Tim saw the video, and Jack's explosion of words took off from there.

If you'd asked me that day, in all my seven months of mothering wisdom and experience, what life would be like for Jack, I wonder what I would have said. I already knew he was alert, cuddly, adorable, and intense. But there was so much I didn't yet know. I couldn't have guessed then that his interests would lean toward trains and books over football and roughhousing. That he would be a great actor. I was just there to see how things unfolded, to witness his personality bloom. But if you had asked me then, I wonder if I would have assumed life would come as easily to Jack as his first word did?

We enter the packed church sanctuary, heading to the front row. In our church you sit in the front row only if you are very late and all the other seats are taken, or if you are the family members at a funeral. Our family's regular Sunday spot is up above on the right side of the balcony. There Jack and Margaret had a clear view of the preacher, and everyone in the church could easily see if it had been a good or bad morning in the Donaldson house depending on how late we traipsed in or whether the kids had sour looks on their faces.

There are more than a thousand people here, with people jammed in the foyer and along the walls. Someone directs latecomers to walk right up onto the platform in front where the choir usually sits. Watching them file in, young and old, makes my heart seize in my chest with gratitude, because I'll be able to look at their faces throughout the service. A stunning picture of Jack stands on the communion table next to his favorite Yankees hat. He's eleven years old in it. Frozen in time. Time already marches ahead, leaving our image of Jack a little boy. The room is full of flowers.

Love and pain course through the church. People from all aspects of our lives come to support us. Kids in baseball, soccer, and school uniforms sit next to church members whom I've known since I was a little girl. Tim's and my cousins from around the country. High school and college friends we haven't seen in twenty years. Colleagues from our current and former jobs. My sister's and brother's friends who have driven five hours to support them. Neighbors. Strangers. Elderly relatives battling cancer, who will hang on to life just a few months longer themselves. What will the service be like for them, to consider a young, unblemished, healthy boy heading to the next life before they do? I'm awed by how so many people show up at great inconvenience to themselves to support our broken, hurting family.

Our two pastors speak, and dear friends from church play guitars and sing beautiful, hopeful songs about heaven. We've asked Jack's friend Gracie if she'd be willing to read an e-mail she sent to Jack on Friday after the accident. I hope she didn't mind that I always read my kids' e-mails. With bravery and poise she says:

Dear Jack,

This is Gracie from DCS. I never got to say bye to you or see you since last summer's end of the year dance, so I'll say what I would say. I've never met someone as funny as you, Jack, and I never will. You are very creative; you boggle my mind when you make these fantastic poems, drawings, sayings, buildings out of Legos, and stories. Your laugh is contagious, and I can still hear it in the back of my head. I'm so sorry that this was all the time on earth that you had, but that time with you was great. Sometimes when I was lonely and left out, we would talk to each other. Of course you were never lonely because you were so popular and everyone loved you, even people in younger and older classes. I'm really going to miss you, Jack, and I can't process in my brain what has happened. Just know that you are loved. I know you are having a great time in your Legoland castle with God, and are having a contest of who can make each other laugh first or kill the most spiders.

I love you, Gracie.

Tim sobs into my shoulder. Margaret sits stoically next to us in the pew. That scares me more than the crying. She seems so small and strong and reminds me so much of myself. The children's principal speaks of Jack's acting ability, faith in God, fast speech, intelligence, and his humility. Cousin Mark reads words written by Liz, highlighting the six lessons she'd learned from Jack, and that would continue to inspire her for the rest of her life:

Be Kind

Pay Attention

Think

Never Give Up
Play
Share Others' Joy
Liz captures his quick mind, attention to detail, and huge heart with her words. Then, my brother, John, reads Jack's own words to us:

A Psalm of Thanksgiving
by Jack Donaldson

God, You are good,
Your Goodness extends beyond the bonds of eternity.
God, You have done great things,
Helping many in times of need.
God, You have done great things for me,
You have helped me in times of struggle.
God, You are merciful,
Sacrificing Your only Son for our life.
God, You are powerful,
You reign supreme over all the nations.
God, You care about me.
Your love endures forever.

When my turn comes, Cindy is on standby to read for me if necessary. Her quiet, steady presence at my elbow will not flag in the days and months to come. But somehow we both know I'll read Jack's eulogy myself. I've been speaking up for Jack since he was born. I look out at the faces of those come together in dread and pain, to honor a sweet boy who was torn violently away. I take a few seconds to scan the church, letting the moment sink in as best I can, then begin.

As I read the words I've written, I feel filled with the Holy Spirit. It's as if I can speak forever, and I want to. I am full of light and energy. I want to run to the rear of the church and lock the doors, keeping us here for all time, remembering Jack and what made him special, and talking about God and eternal things.

In that moment I am sure of the hope of heaven, and I don't want anyone to leave until they are too. I don't want them to go and resume normal life, for how can life be normal after what has happened? I feel my love for Jack and his for me flowing through me, and I am somehow aware that God is working through what I'm saying as my mouth moves and I hear myself speak.

I share that Jack, the truth teller, would not want to be portrayed as perfect. That none of us is perfect and the good news is we don't have to be. I speak of Jack's great love of home, and that he is now in a better home than we could ever imagine. These are incredibly difficult words for me to say, knowing that my goal as a mother is to provide a loving home for my children, but as I say them, I know they are true.

Later, I'll lament to Tim that there was so much more to say about Jack that I'd forgotten, but while I'm speaking, it feels as if God is using the words in a way that reaches beyond the simple little stories of home and life I share. I hope those listening get a glimpse of Jack, and God, and will somehow be changed.

I can feel God's Spirit in the sanctuary, and carrying us through the receiving line, as we comfort those who had come to comfort us. Seeing us standing upright gives our friends a glimmer of hope that parents can survive everyone's worst nightmare, although at just three days in, we don't yet know this is truth. Then, as we had done more than once a week for a lifetime, we exit the side door of the church to head home. This time without Jack.

II

impossible

thirteen

I wonder how much to share. I want to be honest about what the first days of early grief are like, yet I don't want to be cruel. That's why I don't think I can move forward in this story if I don't first tell you what happens when I eventually see Mrs. Davidson in the grocery store.

The grocery store is the absolute worst, most hellish place for me to be after Jack's accident. Far worse than seeing the ridiculous, empty joke of a creek every day or driving over the drainpipes or sitting on his bed surrounded by his things but with no Jack. Or even church, where my raw emotions are right on the surface, always, threatening to pour out when I'm just trying to make it through the hour and get back to my car.

The grocery store trumps them all.

When you spend years trying to get two underweight, picky eaters to eat something, anything, every section holds a memory. The dairy case reminds me of the years when all they wanted to eat was cheese. Chicken noodle soup reminds me of tummy bugs and, later, sore teeth from braces. Dill pickles remind me of the time Jack and I froze the pickle juice left in the jar to make a giant "picklesicle" for him. I stagger through the aisles, throwing things in the cart, the pain leaking out in tears, as I try to figure out how to shop for our new reality. It's where I buy Old Spice body wash for a boy who no longer needs it. I'll wash myself with it every day, just so I can smell him sometimes.

Yet this place of pain is also where, months after the accident, I see my childhood neighbor, Mrs. Davidson. Her son Kenny died in a car accident at age nineteen, over twenty years ago when I was away at college. I recognize her instantly from her jet-black hair and bright red lipstick. It's as if she hasn't aged at all, while I feel like I'm at least 150 years old.

I'm nervous about saying something, but I know, just know, that I must ask her a question. I'm afraid she won't remember me or won't have heard about

Jack, and I'll have to tell her about the accident, right here in the middle of Giant Foods.

But in the cereal aisle, burdened by Frosted Mini-Wheats and Reese's Puffs, but emboldened by desperation and pain, I stop Mrs. Davidson and re-introduce myself to her. She has heard about Jack. I tell her I have a question. "I just have to know. Does it get better?" Without hesitating for even a second, Mrs. Davidson answers, "Oh yes!" I think, even in my shattered condition, I would be able to see through her if she's lying to me. Her answer is quick. Confident. Assured.

It's not as if she says it is easy, surviving the death of a child. I'm not stupid enough to ask her that and would call bullshit if anyone dared try to convince me that "easy" is even possible. But there she is, still coloring her hair and putting on her signature lipstick after all these years. Still grocery shopping, which I now know should never be taken for granted. And she confidently asserts that it does get better.

Mrs. Davidson and I are not close. I doubt that we'll ever see each other again, but I need to share her "Oh yes!" right now because if we are going to look at what the days and months are like following Jack's death, spending time with these snapshots of grief, if we are going to take brave steps together into the confusion of losing what we love the most, doesn't it help to hear from the outset that somehow, in some way, it does get easier?

And it's true. I can assure you, looking back on those days and months now, it does get better.

But not before it gets worse.

As I write about what those days and weeks are like, the *what* seems less important than the *how*. How does one wake up the next day and the next? How do you force yourself to breathe and to eat when both seem disgusting and ridiculous? How do you keep from losing your mind? How do you live knowing the dirty secret that most moms try to stave off as long as possible if they ever face it at all—that control is an illusion?

Because despite my attempts to follow my mother's example and relax and trust God with my kids, I'd clung to a belief that I could somehow control our futures if I just tried hard enough. And if my solo efforts weren't enough, there was always God. Surely God could see how we wanted to live our lives for Him. How we had formed our family around loving and serving Him. And praying.

Jack was well prayed for. That he would be healthy and grow. That he would make true friends. That others could see in him what we did. That he would know his own worth. Prayers of courage. Prayers of protection. Was it all a crock?

We made sure we were in church every single week. Not because we believed in getting credit for good behavior, but because we wanted our kids to understand our house was built on something bigger than ourselves, on the solid rock of God, not the shifting sand of money, status, or busyness that was so valued in our society.

Now I can't shake the image we have on video of three-year-old Jack singing his Sunday school song with motions, some of his *r*'s coming out more like *w*'s in his little-boy voice: "The wain came down and the floods came up. The wain came down and the floods came up. The wain came down and the floods came up, and the house on the rock stood firm."

How will our house stand in this flood?

fourteen

In these early days sleep isn't much of an escape, even though we all crawl into bed as early as eight thirty. Before, it was rare for me to turn in before midnight. But grief is so exhausting.

Just as a mother is attuned to the smallest sounds from her newborn, or the way she wakes immediately when a barefoot, older child pads next to her side of the bed on the verge of throwing up, I remain on high alert even in sleep. I must be ready this time! Adrenaline surges through my panicked body until I realize, again, that I'm seconds too late.

Most nights Tim sleeps soundly, getting some relief from his heartbreak, and maybe even getting to dream of Jack. Margaret rolls and rotates, sometimes lodging a little foot in my face, forcing my head onto the pointy edge of the nightstand. Our family has shrunk, and so has our world, down to just a few rooms and one bed.

I want her to feel comforted, squeezed in between us, the parents who are charged with protecting her and making her feel safe. I don't know if having her in our bed will affect Tim's and my relationship, but it is hard to care about anything other than our loss and our struggle to survive right now.

We understand why Margaret doesn't want to sleep on another floor that she'd shared with her now-dead brother. Up the stairs, her bright aqua room sits unused next to his lime-green one, filled with Legos and signs of an unfinished life. Her messy sink next to his neat one in the bathroom. Later, Tim and I will ask the grief therapist we start seeing every two weeks if it's okay that Margaret shares our bed.

"Absolutely. She'll decide when to go back upstairs and sleep by herself. She needs the security now."

One morning I wake up, reach for my blue bathrobe, and head into the tiny bathroom. Looking in the mirror at eyes that seem old and empty, I realize the initial shock is starting to wear off, and the horror of reality—a future without Jack—is starting to set in.

My most painful memory around my mother's death was the knowledge that she registered for her first passport in her early forties and never got to use it. It seemed there would be time to travel later, but there wasn't. Because of this, part of my dream was to travel with my family someday. I imagined big holiday celebrations, beach trips, and cruises with my children and, eventually, grandchildren.

Today, staring at the face in the mirror, I think of all those years when I tried to put one foot in front of the other and choose joy because I knew that would honor my mother and God. I smiled. I loved. I thrived. I learned there are many, many things one can and will get through without the help of a mom, even though it's hard.

But now, I don't know how I'll keep going. What if I live another forty years? The possibility makes me sick. But in order to make Margaret feel safe, I must take care of her. So I know I must make a pact with the woman in the mirror, something to tether me to a world where I don't want to be: *I will not kill myself today.*

It doesn't mean I want to live without Jack. I don't. It doesn't mean I'm okay with what has happened. I'm not. I must do it for Margaret. I don't know what this day will hold, but it's got to be worth *something* to know that one option is completely, utterly off the table.

And Jack's passport? It sits on the desk in Tim's office. Not a frickin' stamp on it.

fifteen

It's clear in the early aftermath of Jack's death that Tim, Margaret, and I will handle our grief differently. If *handle* is even the word. *Endure? Approach?*

A day or two after the accident, Tim and his dad sit out on the screened porch playing cribbage in the warm weather. I know men like to be doing something, instead of just sitting around talking. But playing cards seems off to me. Like the day after the funeral when Tim, his parents, and his brother go into Washington, DC, to visit museums and see an IMAX movie. Within a week *Smithsonian* magazine shows up in our mailbox.

"Did you order this?" I ask Tim, pulling it from the massive stack of sympathy cards and Jack's latest Lego magazine.

"Yeah, if I became a Smithsonian member, our movie tickets were cheaper," he says. I drop it on the kitchen table like it's a viper. I can't picture going to a museum, let alone comparison shopping for a deal on movie tickets, at a time like this. I'll throw the magazine in the recycling bin each month when it arrives, annoyed that it represents one more difference I'll have to learn to navigate in our new lives. It quickly becomes clear to me that Tim needs distraction and activity.

I'm not surprised by Tim's and my differences in grief, because we've always been different. I am outgoing and irreverent, a fast talker prone to oversharing and laziness. I am a noticer of details and people. I can tell when someone feels left out or needs a hug, and I still remember what my best friend wore to school on the first day of eighth grade. Tim is introverted and quiet, a structured, steady hard worker who avoids crude humor and gives people the benefit of the doubt. He's not good with names or faces but is always modest and kind; his booming voice and big laugh come as a surprise when he does decide to speak.

We're so different that when we try to fold a blanket together, I'll ask myself, *How would I fold this?* and then do the opposite, knowing Tim's approach to absolutely everything is the reverse of mine. Don't even get me started on how he loads a dishwasher. Why wouldn't we be so different with handling grief?

I am infinitely grateful for one way in which Tim and I are different. He does not blame me for Jack's death. I mean, I will always be the one who let the kids play outside in the rain. It's hard for me to understand how Tim could ever forgive me for that. I'm afraid that if the tables were turned, I would be poisoned against him forever. But when I apologize, over and over, he looks at me as if I'm crazy to even say "I'm sorry." He offers up to me gracious words that I barely believe, but that I must accept in order to survive and ever be able to look him in the eyes. "How do you know I wouldn't have let them play in the rain if I'd been home?" he says. "It could have happened to anyone."

Margaret's first reactions to her brother's death remind me so much of myself when my mother died. Smiling, achieving, moving forward, but hurting on the inside. She can easily say Jack's name in conversation and spend hours looking at his photos and drawings, but she doesn't cry, and her feelings about the night of the accident are off-limits. She is resolute in her refusal to speak of it. It's as if she does, she will shatter into a million pieces.

A few weeks after the accident, Margaret becomes anxious. She's afraid of getting sick, being robbed, kidnapped, or dying. And any sign of discord stresses her out, even if Tim and I are just talking about our schedule for the week or debating if Shadow needs to go out to pee. I think it's just one more way she doesn't feel anything's certain anymore. A simple cough could be whooping cough. One beer could be the path to alcoholism. One argument can lead to divorce. If Mom starts to cry, what if she can't stop? And Margaret doesn't have her best friend to share the burden with, because he's the reason she found out about the uncertainty of life in the first place.

"Of course we'll keep you safe" rings hollow when the three of us now know there are no guarantees. She doesn't trust our judgment as parents anymore, and I don't blame her.

I vow not to sink so far into my own grief that I can't parent her in the way she needs, but what does that even mean? She needs good mothering more than ever before, but I am depleted. Do I have what it takes to help her know that Alive Margaret is not less important than Dead Jack? My sadness frightens her, because when you are ten and your brother has vanished, the last thing you want to do is lose your mother to the blackness of grief. When I cry or talk about my grief, it makes her world seem even less secure, and it's already hanging by a thread.

It's for Margaret that I decide not to touch a drop of alcohol for at least the first three months. I'm not much of a drinker at all, but I can see myself taking one drink and another, then climbing right inside the bottle. I don't want to give her one more thing to worry about.

Even though my sadness scares her, I know acting as though everything is fine won't help one bit either, because it's not the truth, so I give her metered glimpses of my grief, while still trying to appear as stable as possible. She watches every move. It's important to her that I still pack her lunch and that the laundry is done. That I drive the carpool. That I know who the people are on reality TV. Neither of us mentions that I play the same praise CD on a loop in the car over and over and over.

Margaret misses only three days of school after the funeral, bravely climbing out of the car to walk into the tiny building alone. Her new classroom is Jack's from last year. His friends sit at a table just a few rows from her own in the cafeteria. She throws herself into fifth grade, her work neat, meticulous, and organized. She makes her classmates laugh with her wit, exuberance, and energy, and she faces off against the boys in soccer at recess. Without realizing it, she's helping the other children. Margaret models survival, which is interesting because she's so worried and we are so worried about her.

I wonder if, as her classmates grow and face the inevitable losses and crushing blows of life, they will remember a spunky girl in a navy plaid skirt and sneakers and think, *If Margaret Donaldson did it, I can too.*

Margaret tells me she sometimes imagines that at the end of the day, Jack will dash past her, throw open the car door, and climb into his seat, forcing her to climb over him, like he used to do. Instead, she stands alone in their spot in front of the school. She opens the door herself, hoists her heavy backpack onto Jack's seat, and climbs over it into her own. His seat is closer, but she won't sit there. I wonder how many times a day she still stops to think, as I do, *Did this really happen?* It seems so shocking, impossible, and weird. Can someone be gone, dead, when his favorite cereal is in the pantry? School clothes lined up on a shelf? When he still gets mail?

I do some imagining too. I try to be one of the first cars in the carpool line, figuring that if I'm this tired, Margaret must be exhausted and more than ready to come home. Jack's class is finishing PE in the field in front of the school. If I squint my eyes, there's just a sea of navy and khaki in front of me. It's easy to imagine Jack there, lunging for a ball, falling into a funny pratfall that turns into a roll, the boys and girls laughing. I want to stay like this forever, imagining he is only feet from me. Imagining that life is as it was. But when my eyes clear, I can see Davis's blond head, with no brown-haired Jack standing almost a foot shorter, next to him, where he belongs. The picture seems awkward, incomplete, and my eyes cloud again, this time with tears. How will I breathe when his best friends get facial hair, and when their voices change? When they move on without Jack?

These nine kids are the ones who yelled good-bye and raced to carpool on a wet Thursday afternoon as their friend Jack finished stacking chairs for the PE sub. They never saw him again. Now, each afternoon they come to my car. I don't know it yet, but they will show up 181 school days in a row, even in the rain. As they line up and hug me through the window, I try not to act greedy or needy. I am starved for a touch from Jack's people, his tribe. I will learn to have a piece of gum or a mint to offer, a tiny token for the bravery they show by coming to my window day after day.

I suppose they need to see that if Jack's mom is going to make it, so will they, despite the pain, the questions, and the fears that have bubbled up in them. I hate that their love for Jack has thrust them into a world of uncertainty, making our pain their pain too. I try not to cry. I try to wear work clothes instead of sweats and put on makeup. They tell me Jack stories they've thought of in advance, holding them up and offering them to me as precious jewels. We laugh. Each story matters, because we are beginning to realize there is a finite supply.

Tim and I return to work less than two weeks after the accident; he to his law office and I to the church bookstore. We can't think of any other options, so we go. None of us knows how to act. I assume that everyone who looks at us is thinking about Jack and shares in our misery, but few people say anything at all. They just so fervently, so intensely, want us to be all right.

My colleagues smile and say, "Hi, Anna. How are you today?" and I'm thinking, *How the hell do you think I am?* I refuse to answer "Fine" because I think it's a cop-out and does nothing to tell the truth about grieving. But what should I say? I don't want to make an awkward situation worse, so I usually get by with a small tight-lipped smile and a shrug of my shoulders, or I'll say, "I'm hanging in." Could anyone even handle the ugly truth?

A few hours before the accident, my colleague Melissa and I were chatting in the copy room upstairs. "Get ready. Jack's going to get a lot of attention from youth group girls this year," she said. "Seriously? He's too shy," I replied. "Oh, he will. You're in big trouble, Anna!" We laughed, thinking of Jack becoming a ladies' man. Now Melissa stops by my office every week or so to see how I'm coping.

A few women I've known forever, and others who have reached out since the accident, come by the store to give me a hug among the bookshelves or bring me a smoothie or a cup of tea. We sit by my desk, look at each other with shocked expressions, and cry. Sometimes we talk. I'm grateful that they, clueless and scared, will venture into the grief with me.

It dawns on me that I've never walked beside someone in deep pain. I've been more of a drive-by friend, the kind who reaches out once or twice and hopes the situation will be resolved quickly. I care. I cry. I pray. But I don't stick around long. I'm the type of friend you would want around for a broken ankle but not for chronic depression. I get a sense I'm learning from the women who show up for me. Who offer themselves up in a way that I've never had the guts to do. They are braver than they think.

sixteen

Walking into our church building the morning of the accident, I to the bookstore and Tim to the basement to meet with the youth pastor about volunteering, was as natural for us as entering our own home. But now, church is weird. The basement where the teen activities take place feels off-limits, our regular seats in the balcony feel overexposed to sympathetic eyes, and even my office, where Jack would hang out each week after Sunday school, seems dark and grim. It is incomprehensible to be here without Jack in his khakis and orange-and-white-striped polo, tugging my arm, telling me it's time to go home.

Our ministers, who are also our friends, feel at a loss to minister to us. They, too, struggle with what happened. Jack's death has rocked our church community, and though they've poured out their love to us, we still feel like outsiders here, in the land of organ music, Sunday school classes, programs, and meetings.

It is as if what we're going through is almost too real and too raw to bring up at church. But if you can't bring up matters of life and death and God's Spirit here, where can you? Maybe it's because we are accustomed to dealing with issues in tidy chunks. We grapple, but we do it during a twenty-minute sermon, a twelve-week class, a topic scheduled six to eight months in advance. There is nothing tidy about a child dying.

I remember walking into church the first Sunday after the 9/11 terrorist attacks. My best friend, Diana, whom I've known since we were five years old, said, "Gol, look at how full it is! Why is it so crowded?" And I knew. I got a glimpse then, like I'm getting a glimpse now, that when the world seems to shift, either for millions and millions the way it did in September 2001 or for our little family and our friends in September 2011, we turn our hearts and questions to God, looking for comfort and answers.

How I want to talk about where God is in all of this! I want to share some of the strange and miraculous things He did before the accident and in the days since, like Margaret's premonition about Jack dying and the Bible verses popping up on my phone, but I don't know where or even how to bring it up. Do I add it to the agenda at our weekly staff meeting? Surely people would listen, but would I look too vulnerable and needy? Do I stand on a box in the middle of the hallway like some unhinged prophet in the town square?

I am relieved to have just finished my term on our church leadership board, because if I were still serving on it, I'm afraid I'd stand up and say something rude at a meeting, that I'd be a loose cannon. We'd be talking budgets and programs and ministries and the church calendar, all things that formerly interested me.

But in my grief, everything seems meaningless if it doesn't deal with life and death and the promise of heaven. I can picture myself standing up, yelling, "This is all bullshit!" "What about the miracles?" "What about angels?" "Isn't our God the same God as in the Bible?" "Why do we keep acting like we are *in charge of anything*?" I would look crazy, make my friends feel uncomfortable, and probably say the F word. Losing steam, I would whisper, finally, the questions my heart is really asking, "How could God possibly think it was a good idea to take Jack?" and "Can we even trust Him anymore?"

The youth workers counsel the middle and high schoolers in their grief. They tell me that it has never been easier to get right to the spiritual, heart issues with the kids. They want to open up and talk, to question and to wonder.

But what about the rest of the church? Is Jack's death going to be just another sad story, a blip next to concerns about worship styles and staffing? Even in my shocked state, it's clear to me that God is on the move through Jack's death. I am able to recognize this because the inconsequential, everyday concerns that have always distracted me have fallen away in the wake of the accident. I'm not sure how long this will last, and I don't want to squander anything I'm learning. It needs to be shared.

But I am a most unlikely person for the role. For I have neither the stamina nor the inclination to proclaim any new revelations. I am tired. I am hurting. I don't feel like being God's cheerleader. And what's the point of sharing anyway, when this knowledge has come at so high a price? That living our lives as if we are in control is an illusion? Won't every person who lives be able to learn these truths on his own, through the inevitable losses to come?

Some will learn suddenly as we have, and others will learn slowly over time. I think of Margaret, who didn't have the luxury of learning about loss as an adult or in a gradual, natural way. At an age when being even the slightest bit different is a burden, she feels different in a significant way. If I could, I would take that burden from her. I'd carry it in a sack with me, alongside my own grief and pain, until she reached adulthood. Until she'd had a chance to experience other losses—of a pet, a friendship, first love, of a dream or two. I'd let it out slowly, in metered doses, so it could settle gently around her shoulders and not knock her to the ground.

So I keep my mouth shut at church. I go to work in the bookstore. I order intellectual books about ten steps to grow closer to God. About how to study the Bible. About prayer. About the Holy Spirit. I place the books on the shelves, for people to read and experience privately in their homes. It's all very neat and predictable. And I guess that's part of the problem. The God I've been experiencing since Jack's death is real and anything but predictable. The trappings of church feel stale and representational by comparison.

We keep going, though, sitting in our usual spot up in the balcony. I try to open my mouth to sing, but when I do, my eyes fill with tears and my mouth snaps shut again like a marionette. Instead, I dig my fingernails into my palms to try to keep the tears from spilling onto my cheeks. The hymns are about God's power, tenderness, and faithfulness, all of which I've experienced first-hand in my pain. I have felt His Spirit in me, even on that horrible night. But I just can't sing along with the choir. I just can't offer my praises to Him in the pain. I tell God that I'm going to keep showing up and looking for Him, but my days of trying hard are over.

Weeks from now, our communion coordinator will ask if I'm ready to start serving communion again during worship. "I can barely take communion now, let alone serve it," I answer bluntly. The intimacy with God through communion implies that all is right in our relationship, and I'm not sure about that.

The truth is I'm trying to settle into a new relationship with God, in light of what has happened to my boy. I've never felt more loved by God in my life or held so closely by Him—almost as if I'm wrapped in soft, cotton batting. It is this inexplicable feeling of love, coupled with my responsibility to Margaret, that helps keep me from giving up. But I've never felt so disappointed and hurt either. I'm recalibrating our relationship, and the only broken body I can picture right now is Jack's.

seventeen

W hat if heaven is boring, Mom?"
"Eternity seems like way too long to be in any one place."
"*Forever* scares me."

Jack was afraid of heaven.

We would talk about it at bedtime, and I wondered if I was the best person to calm his fears. Sure, I wanted to go to heaven someday, but I couldn't imagine it being all that great. I'm not musical, so choirs of angels don't appeal to me. Streets of gold and jewels? Ick. Over-the-top opulence struck me as gaudy—a cheesy amusement park gone wrong.

And the idea of constant worship freaked me out too. It has always been hard for me to truly let go and worship God. In fact, one of the easiest times for me to really get into worship, swaying, clapping, and calling out to Him, happened to be at a retreat in Indiana—a plane ride away from anyone I might know. I guess you could say the idea of holding up my arms in the air or falling on my face in worship makes me mildly uncomfortable, so I didn't relish the idea of doing it for all eternity.

And then there was my mom. It was a hard sell for me to believe there could be any better place for a forty-six-year-old woman than with her kids, on earth, where they needed her. She was the heart of our home, and home was where she belonged.

And what if heaven was too formal for her? She loved Jesus—the dusty-footed, sinner-loving Jesus. Would heavenly Jesus be a little too...stuffy for her? She liked to dig her hands in the dirt, eat half a pound of gumdrops in one sitting, throw back her head and laugh, and screw up the punch line of the only joke she knew. Can you even do those things in heaven?

After she died it was as if a steel wall came down between the two of us, between here and there. Heaven felt so far away. I saw no signs indicating she was okay. I felt no closeness, just absence and lack. I did not comfort myself knowing we would see each other again someday, because I wasn't sure if that's even how it worked. I didn't want to get my hopes up, only to be disappointed later.

Fortunately, I didn't dump all of this on Jack, but I just listened in his bed in the dark to his concerns, which were similar to my own. We read a few books about children who had gone to heaven and come back. That helped. So did a conversation he had with a camp counselor when he was ten. "I'm not afraid of heaven anymore," he announced as we debriefed after his week away. I got no more details, but I was relieved. Jack was now fine with heaven. But that didn't really change my own views.

In the few weeks since Jack's death I've gone from being someone who rarely thought about heaven to someone living with one foot here and the other there. My kid is in heaven. I don't need to know the nitty-gritty, like how big it is, where it is, or absolutely everything you do there. But I need to know something! I never even let Jack go to a sleepover if I didn't know the family well and what he could expect there. But now he's somewhere very, very different, and I don't really know what it's like.

And here's the strange thing. Heaven is central to our belief as Christians. We believe that Christ offers us eternal life in heaven, but in my almost four decades in church, I've rarely heard anything about what heaven is like. Aren't we curious? Why are our minds not being blown by the fact that a soul can live forever with God? Do we consider ourselves too intellectual to consider the spiritual realm? And if so, why do we bother saying we have faith in the first place, when to have faith is to believe in something we cannot see? Are we so rooted in the here and now that we treat heaven just as some insignificant, distant reward?

I'm pretty clueless about heaven, and even though I want Jack's new home to be better than anything he could experience here, I have a hard time accepting how it could be better than life with us.

In October, I write on my blog:

Heaven had better be:
  Better than any stinkin' Youth Group costume party.
  And being trapped inside a Lego Factory over a long weekend with
    plenty of Cheez-Its and Dr Pepper.
  And the buzzy feeling you get when the person you have a crush on
    crushes on you back.
  And sledding down a huge hill with your best friends until it's cocoa
    time.
  And a wonderful, fumbly first kiss.
  And skiing black diamonds with your dad in Colorado.
  And a high school debate trip to New York City with fun but
    slightly lax chaperones.
  And praising God at a retreat and finally getting how much He
    loves you.
  And sitting around with your friends at college laughing until your
    stomach hurts.
  And falling in love.
  And watching in person as the Yankees win the World Series…
    again!
  And surprising your little sister by flying in for her college
    graduation.
  And doing work that fulfills you and honors God.
  And dancing with your mom at your wedding.
  And holding your newborn baby—staring at your wife thinking,
    "We made this?"
  And giving that baby a bath and zipping him up in footy pajamas.
  Oh yeah, and sex.
  Heaven had better be more wonderful than sex.
  Okay, God? Good.

Although I write almost daily, sharing my grief in real time on my blog, I'm having difficulty reading the newspaper, a magazine, or a book. My brain feels too shocked and fractured to translate the words into something coherent. And I don't want to waste my time or effort on anything if it can't somehow help me.

The first book I manage to get through is a compilation of the grief stories of a dozen bereaved parents. They speak candidly about the shock, anger, and sadness of losing a child. I'm hoping these parents' stories show me that our family will somehow endure. I need to know, because it doesn't feel like an assumption I can readily make.

One person in the book grates on me so much, however, that I'm tempted to skip his sections. He's a dad who lost his young son in a freak accident, much like Jack's. I can't understand or relate to him as he writes about connecting to his son on a "soul level" and about their ongoing relationship after his son's death. I find him tiresome and grasping. It seems to me that grief has turned him into a total fruitcake.

I fret. What are his words doing to bereaved parents who never feel their children's presence with them? Who don't connect to their kids in the way he talks about? What will his words do to me? Will I be tormented that my Jack seems so far away, even though this guy says his son is so close? Isn't he intensifying our pain?

I worry that this man can't accept that his son is dead and isn't coming back. Haven't we all heard that acceptance is important, a stage not to be missed? If we don't face the fact that our kids are really gone, won't we be trapped in some sort of "grief limbo" forever? I'm a reluctant pupil, forced into a course of studies I detest, but I know I don't want to somehow fail this class and have to take it all over again.

I can barely pray when I read this book, but I send up a thought to God: *Please don't make me end up like this guy.*

eighteen

I get hundreds of messages from friends and strangers telling me the impact Jack's death has had on them, in many cases making them more loving, attentive mothers who hold their children closer and take the time to really be present with them. It has been a wake-up call about how fleeting life is.

And shouldn't we *all* become better people, because we know what's important now? Isn't that the lesson when someone we love dies? To cherish life? To love and appreciate one another, because we realize the time we have together is a gift?

But that's not really what I'm seeing play out in my house. I don't suddenly turn into some grace-filled, holy woman just because something horrific happened to my child. To think so would be as simplistic as thinking all moms whose kids have cancer are somehow braver than everybody else. Or that no mother with a multiply handicapped child can be a raging bitch. We are human. We are flawed. We are ordinary people thrust into less than ordinary situations, just doing what we have to do.

I'm far from perfect, even with my new perspective. I feel great love and I love, but I'm also irritable and overwhelmed. The sound of Tim chewing his cereal makes me want to crawl out of my skin just as it always has, even though I now know he could get hit by a bus tomorrow. Can't I show him grace in the little things when he has shown me grace in the biggest thing of all, by not blaming me for letting the kids play in the rain? But Tim's no beacon of sweetness and light either. He is short with me and defensive. And I can't figure out the best way to relate to Margaret, as she swats away my hand or wriggles away from me when I try to pull her close.

It dawns on me that another injustice of loss is that it's easier for others to talk about and process the loss of Jack than those of us who have lost the most.

They can gather at bus stops, over a meal, or in small groups to try to make sense of it. For those of us who fully realize what we have lost in losing Jack, not just *a* son and brother, but *our* son and brother, the pain is so deep it scares us to approach it fully. To try to give voice to our feelings, our longings for him, and our fears for the future seems too primal to put into words. Instead, our sadness comes out in small irritations and slights.

Mealtimes are tense. I think of family dinners past, some of which were wonderful, some of which were horrendous. I remember one in particular, when dinner was spinning out of control. Jack gagged on his broccoli, using his dramatic skills to their full extent. The microscopic piece of broccoli ended up on the floor. Margaret spit whatever she was eating into her nice cloth napkin and kept putting a dirty, bare foot right on the table. Any attempt at civilized conversation failed.

I could tell from the look in Tim's eyes that he wondered why he'd busted his butt to come home to *this*. After the kids left the table to run around outside, Tim looked at me and, using a rare curse word, said, "I'm worried we're raising assholes."

"Well, I'm around kids all day, every day," I replied. "Dude, they're all assholes."

And now I yearn for more ridiculous dinners like that one—bad manners, dirty feet, curse words, and all.

Instead, we sit in a triangle around the table, eating food prepared by friends and left in a cooler by the kitchen door. I try to train myself to reach for only three plates in the cupboard, but muscle memory is wired from more than a decade of reaching for four. I must remind myself each night: three, not four.

I sit alone under the window on the bench that Jack and Margaret used to share. Margaret has moved over into my seat, without a word. We hold hands, which now involves a long, awkward diagonal reach, and we sing a halfhearted "God is great, God is good, and we thank Him for our food." Margaret starts whining about something, sounding more like a four-year-old than a ten-year-old. I can tell Tim's frustration is starting to build, because the two veins on his forehead—nicknamed the Tigris and Euphrates—begin to bulge. Dinner is going downhill fast.

I'm already in my flannel pajamas and bathrobe, and it's not even six o'clock. Despite my exhaustion from living through the day, I swoop quickly into emotion-interpreter mode.

Avoiding all eye contact, I say to my plate, in a formal but neutral way, "I wonder if Margaret is getting tired of eating food that other families have cooked for us. With all the changes in our lives, it's just one more thing she has no control over. And I wonder if Daddy is frustrated that we can't eat dinner in peace without any crying and complaining. I wonder if he's worried that every single dinner from now on will be like this."

No one says anything in response, but the tension disappears. We eat.

Jack was a great emotional decoder. I think of the time a few weeks before the accident when he quietly cornered me in the upstairs hallway on a night Margaret had a friend sleeping over. "Alexis is a year older than Margaret, and you're making them go to bed too early. I think that's going to embarrass her." He was right, but I hadn't noticed a thing.

Jack seemed to have such insight into our moods, talking me down off the ledge and trying to explain to young Margaret that parents get angrier and yellier the later at night it gets, so if they were going to act up, earlier was definitely better. I need him here to help us with all of this!

But we try the best we can without him. We look at clues for one another's methods of coping, even though we don't understand them. We try to decode what God's purpose could be in giving us signs of warning before, and comfort after, but not bothering to save our son. We try to figure out how to act normal enough to make Margaret feel safe, while not pretending everything is okay. Because it's not. The reality is, we just miss Jack. Our lives feel unnatural. We are shocked. Bewildered. Sad. Bereft.

We drive back from Margaret's soccer game an hour away. Soccer is the only thing we look forward to on these long, quiet, empty weekends, when church is no longer a refuge but just something we endure. I guess it's good she plays year-round. We have no baseball, no Boy Scouts, no youth group. Tim speeds along the highway and swerves a little, making me reach for the plastic handle above my head. From the backseat we hear Margaret say in a sarcastic voice, "Jack, we're coming! We're coming!" and we all laugh. Laughter has always been one of our family's greatest gifts. And it feels so good.

nineteen

I f I'd made a list of who I thought would be there with us to try to pick up the pieces after a tragedy, that list would have been off. Not way off, but off. And at a time when many, many people sacrifice themselves to be present for us, I may have expected to be surprised but not disappointed.

I soon learn that prior closeness does not determine who will show up for you. My neighbor Jenn and I knew each other less than six months before the accident, but she steps right into our grief with us, showing up physically by helping meet our needs, emotionally, by repeatedly coming into our home instead of keeping a polite distance, and spiritually, when she allows Jack's death to seep into her heart and turn her toward God. When asked why her family attends church and Bible study now, she simply says, "Jack."

Karen, the mother of one of Jack's classmates, knew of Jack mainly from funny stories her daughter told at the dinner table over the years. Our contact was just a wave in the pickup line or some chitchat, minivan to minivan. Now Karen commits to checking on me almost daily and finds ways to memorialize Jack, and she specifically asks me what I'm struggling with the most on a given day so she can direct her prayers. "I want to be your Barnabas, Anna. Your encourager." Karen is in a lot of pain over Jack's death, but she refuses to step away.

In contrast, Mary, one of my best friends for over a decade, is distant and then disappears from my life. I am shocked, confused, and worried. Some days I feel like I'm thinking about Mary even more than Jack, although I know that can't be true. I know Jack's death is hard on my friends. Some aren't sleeping and eating. Others have emergency therapy sessions or must go on medication. Mary, who was closer to Jack than the others, worries me the most because she seems unable to be part of our community of grief, where there is great pain but also the possibility of healing together. Losing her makes the grief worse. I learn that death breaks things, even friendships.

I try to make clear what I need from friends by writing about it on my blog, because I know they are probably almost as confused and scared as I am. I am not asking for people to sit with me in the middle of the night while I weep or come over each day to make sure I don't harm myself, even though I know some would be willing to do that if that's what I needed.

Instead, I am looking for a soft place to land. I want to hear how Jack's death has affected my friends. I want to know if they've ever experienced miracles or signs. I want to go over the afternoon of the accident again, as if discussing what details we know will help my mind grasp how any of this could have happened. I want us to look at one another's faces and cry. To say the F word. To question God. To hear that Jack meant something. It is in the telling and retelling that we work our way through painful territory and gain insight.

No matter what form it takes, it will be a show of real feelings, no matter how tentative, awkward, or bumbling. It will be a willingness to suspend talk of petty concerns for just a moment or even a season. I don't give a shit whose daughter gets the most playing time on the soccer field, where to get a good pedicure, or what anyone thinks of standardized tests. I used to. Perhaps I will again. But not today. *Don't talk about stupid shit. Don't talk about stupid shit,* I try to steer people silently with my brain. It doesn't always work.

I know my friends and I will return to more reciprocal relationships at some point, at least I hope so, because who wants to be only a taker, not a giver? But for me, now is the time to process what has happened with people who care.

Grief is my work right now, and I'm afraid to skirt it or run away from it. Everything I've heard tells me that if I try to stuff it down, deny it, or rush through it, I'm just going to have to deal with it later, and then it will be worse. "Worse" scares the shit out of me.

I'm not sure what it means to "deal with it" anyway. It's not like I'm trying to get over Jack, so if that's what "dealing with it" means, I'm truly not interested. Why would I want to "get over" the brown-eyed boy who taught me how to love and who loved me with his whole heart?

The closest picture I can imagine is that I want to lean toward my grief, as opposed to leaning away from it—contorting myself into painful positions as I make a futile attempt to escape from something hideous that is actually adhered to my body. I can't get away from it, unless my twelve-year-old boy shows up at my kitchen counter eating a taco. I try to stay aware of how I'm feeling in each moment. I still refuse to say "Fine" when people ask how I'm doing, because I don't think faking it does anybody any favors.

Friends who grieve with us have to face their own version of leaning into or dealing with the grief. They run the risk of being overwhelmed by it, pulled into their own form of depression, fear, and bitterness. They risk not being there for their own families as they show up for ours. I wonder if those who have come alongside us feel a burden for us, as if they simply don't have a choice to ignore it or will it away.

Is it Jack's face smiling on my blog the first day of school, one day before he died, that reaches into their hearts and won't let them go? Is it a longstanding friendship with our family? Is it looking at their own children asleep in their beds and leaning down to smell their necks? Or is it just that some people are more naturally suited to show compassion and empathy in hard times while others are not? I don't know, but I am humbled and amazed by each person who steps into the muck. I'm not saying it's easy to be friends with a grieving mother. I don't think it is.

Some people who reach out express a fear that they are overstepping. That our ties to one another until now have been tangential, if they've existed at all, yet still they come. I thank each one with a grateful heart, because she might be the exact person I need in this one lonely moment. To shy away due to questions of intruding or forcing intimacy would deprive both of us from taking part in something holy. For I see holiness in giving and receiving love when there is absolutely nothing that can be fixed, and when there's no exit strategy in sight.

Blog readers question whether it is appropriate to mourn a child across the country, or even halfway around the world, whom they have never met. Their confused husbands will ask them, "Why do you do this to yourself? Why don't you just walk away from the computer if that blog always makes you cry?" But they can't. They won't. They know that writing helps me, so they miraculously commit to read whatever I write so I'll have a reason to keep showing up.

If you had asked me before Jack's accident, I would have told you I was more than happy with my relationships. That I was busy, and I wasn't looking for new friends. But to shut out the possibility of new friendships now because I'm clinging to ones that have slipped away is like trying to cling to Jack. It would be easier to try to hold water in my cupped hands while scaling a mountain peak. I promise myself that I will never again assume that someone's closest friends are meeting their needs in a crisis and that I won't use my own feelings of inadequacy as an excuse to not reach out.

One of the greatest surprises comes in the way our larger community shows up for us. Blue ribbons waving from mailboxes, trees, and fence posts are like a hug on a brutally miserable day. One-line texts that say only "I love you and I'm praying." Cards in the mail. A friend putting his lawn mower in the back of his car a few days after the accident and driving over to mow our lawn after he finishes his own. People who cook for us. Online friends who for my sake invest in getting to know Jack now, even though they won't meet him on earth. Somehow, acknowledgment from the community, rather than making us wallow in our grief, makes us stronger.

But when I think of community, I wonder if it's really necessary for so many to suffer. I mean, Tim, Margaret, and I must suffer because Jack was ours. Grieving is the price we pay for loving him so very much. His smile, his voice, his touch are ours to lose. But what about the sadness that slams a tiny school, descends on a town, and spreads throughout this country and beyond through friends and social media? Is it right to want others to share our pain with us, or is that asking too much?

I really hate to use a drowning analogy. I've been struck with how many hymns, praise songs, and even references to grief refer to drowning, and that's a lot for me to take. Last week Margaret and I counted five songs in a row on our Christian radio station dealing with storms, waves, being pulled under, drowning, and floods. But there is an image that keeps coming to me when I think of community. It is of our little family huddled together out in the middle of a winter pond on very thin ice. It's lonely out there. And the weight of our grief and our longing for Jack are so heavy, bearing down on us, that the pond starts to crack.

Then I see us getting down on our bellies and spreading our arms and legs out, almost as if we are embracing the ice. We can't try to run away from it, or we will surely fall in, so we embrace its cold, hard inhospitable presence. Friends, those we have met and those we may not meet for a long time, spread out too, grabbing on to our hands and our feet, until we've redistributed the weight, making a web or a snowflake pattern that reaches to the far edges of the pond and onto solid ground to keep us safe. Tim, Margaret, and I don't go crashing through. Not this day, at least.

twenty

When Jack was a baby and toddler, he hit all his milestones on time or early. Am I the only mom who got wrapped up in all of that, paying lip service to the fact that every child develops at different rates while secretly hoping that mine would leave all the other kids in the dust? My pride rested on our adorable, brilliant, "perfect" firstborn, whom I paraded around like a circus pony. "Say the ABCs in French, Jack!" I would insist, without the slightest provocation or encouragement, and he would. I must have been an insufferable friend. I was just so proud of him.

Jack complied with being looked upon as the Second Coming in our household as the list of things that came so easily to him grew: talking, potty training, being put in new situations, you name it.

In preschool he delighted his teachers with his early language skills. I remember when they told us he spelled the word *semaphore* one day by sounding it out. Semaphore? I didn't even know what that was. (It's a train thing, by the way.) While some of his classmates were standing in the corner pooping in their Pull-Ups, Jack was already reading.

So blinded was I by his aptitude and my own brilliant parenting, it took me a while to notice the ways in which Jack struggled. For instance, he had certain ways he wanted to do things, and it seemed like he would rather get in trouble for finishing what he was doing, in a precise, just-so way, than do what the teachers asked, when they asked. Getting in trouble seemed out of character for the Jack we knew at home, and we wondered if something else was going on. He also cried a lot and seemed extremely sensitive.

I didn't like seeing Jack struggle. I would get frustrated when he came home with a less-than-stellar report from preschool. Yes, preschool. I hadn't yet come to accept that not only do we not have to be perfect, but we can't be. I hadn't yet realized that each child is different.

I had experienced success in my life up until this point and was driven to similar "success" in raising Jack. I veered from loathing his cruel, heartless preschool teachers (because, of course, that's exactly who goes into preschool teaching, right?) for trying to put my baby in a box, to trying to *will* Jack to fit into that box so that life would be easier for him and especially for me. In the back of my mind, I also wondered if something else could be wrong.

Tim, with his structured personality, leaned toward behavior charts and stickers, rewards and punishments. I wanted Jack to behave simply because it was the right thing to do, and I thought such a mature little guy should understand that. Tim and I brought our own backgrounds and baggage to the table, mixed them with a dose of fear and insecurity, and tossed it all with a big dash of societal expectations. No wonder Jack later referred to himself, only half-jokingly, as our "practice child."

My lowest moments in parenting him stemmed from worrying about what other people thought. I knew Jack was an amazing kid, with a pure heart and a generous nature, but when I took my eyes off what I knew to be true, when I let my pride creep in, I became frustrated and made decisions that weren't best for him.

I'll never forget letting a teenage lifeguard dunk Jack during a swim lesson just because I felt pressured by the swim-team moms standing around me. Of course I knew that was no way to get Jack comfortable with water, but I gave in because I felt as if we were somehow not measuring up. The other kids were going off the high dive, and Jack was still doggie paddling and complaining when water got in his eyes. I wanted him to conform. To be an easy kid. So I gave in. I later apologized to Jack, and it nearly broke my heart to see the confused look he gave me, as if he really couldn't grasp that the mom he knew would have agreed to dunk him. Jack believed in me as a mom even more than I did. And of course he learned to swim on his own timetable. I'm grateful he forgave me that and other parenting mistakes I made.

The upside of parenting a kid who sometimes struggled was that it pointed me toward God and away from my focus on worldly success. It's easy to be caught up in the standards of the world when your kid operates beautifully within the structure of what is normal. You can be the parent who gets riled up on the soccer field and thinks it's funny to yell, jokingly, "Get a goal or there's no dinner for you tonight!"

But when your child is somehow different, you are led far beyond win/loss columns and popularity contests. For some parents it is the realization that their child will never speak or walk on his own. For others it means she may never be able to make a true friend. This new reality will render jokes about "the short bus" completely unacceptable and worries about prom dates and AP classes off the table.

And these challenges often point toward God. Toward issues of the heart. To loving well the child you've been given, not the child you thought you would have. To relying on God when your reserves are too low and accepting forgiveness and grace when you screw up. At least that's how it was with Jack. I had always loved Jack, but as time passed, I had begun to learn how to love him well.

I can't believe I won't have a lifetime to keep doing that.

twenty-one

A lmost every morning before school, the whole first year after Jack's death, Joe walks up our long driveway to Daniel's grandparents' house so he and Daniel can walk to school together. Almost every day, before I've had breakfast or even a single cup of tea, I see both of the boys Jack was playing with during his final moments on earth. They are healthy. He is gone. It's not as if I wish they were dead; I'm just devastated that Jack is. And seeing them alive nearly every single morning intensifies the pain.

The paper shades from the day after the accident are still taped to our kitchen window. This helps a bit, but our houses are on top of each other, and the glass door into the carport gives me a full view of the boys each morning long before I'm ready. Will I ever be ready? They stand only yards away from me as I lean over the counter rushing to make one school lunch, not two.

Pain presses down on me. My bed calls me back, beckoning me to give up on this day before it has truly begun. Seeing them takes me right back to the trauma of standing by the creek, yelling at them to look, desperately scanning for Jack, my brain trying to compute what I am seeing.

Instead of returning to bed, I will drop Margaret off at her school and then head back through town toward the bookstore, where chances are good that I will encounter Joe and Daniel again as they cross the final street on their way to their school. "Please, God, *NO!*" I beg as I see the familiar backpacks, the mops of hair. I stop at the Stop sign, and they step into the crosswalk in front of me. Two sightings before nine.

On mild days, when the fall weather somehow retains a hint of summer and I can almost pretend that the horror of September never happened, I hear kids playing and yelling, riding go-karts in the driveway.

It's not Margaret. She doesn't play outside anymore—not without Jack. They were a team, always together. Some days he would send her on a mission down the driveway to "check the mailbox," a pretense they hoped would drum up neighborhood fun. Or they would climb up into the ironwood tree next to the carport, standing and chatting, until other kids came out and joined them for a game of tag or soccer.

Now, when it's still nice enough to play outside after dinner, Joe and Daniel are the last faces I see in the driveway before I turn out the kitchen lights and head down the half flight of stairs to numb myself with TV and ice cream. First in the morning. Last at night.

Shouldn't repeated contact desensitize me to the pain? Isn't this my own form of exposure therapy? Shouldn't I be able to look at them by now and not be transported back to the scene of the accident? Just as there is much more to Jack than a lost boy and a tragic death, surely there is more to them than that instant when they saw one of their friends be swept away in front of them.

Joe and Daniel have grown very close, their bond likely strengthened by the trauma they experienced together, a trauma no child should go through. I'm sure their families are worried about them and grateful they have each other. I wonder if they're getting help. I wonder if they've been able to talk to anyone about what those final seconds were like. I don't talk to them about it, and I don't plan to. I can't look them in the eyes. I don't want to see them or their families, because to do so just reminds me of my terror by the creek that day and of what they have and we don't.

Our shocked, numb interactions with the boys and their families in those first days, when we exchanged warm hugs and felt something akin to love, have given way to awkwardness and pain. We are all living on top of one another as we stumble about, figuring out how to grieve. This means any trip to my car, the recycle bin, or trash can is a potential encounter with the boys or their families, and my body tenses every time in anticipation. A constant soreness settles into my shoulders.

I am worried about the boys and how they are coping, but my concern for them is small, minuscule really, compared to my own pain and sadness, and that makes me feel even worse. A seed of bitterness has fallen in my heart and taken root. I try to reason with myself. They are children! Of course they must move and laugh and play outside. A child can't sustain a constant state of mourning. And of course they must go to school, but it feels as if Jack's been replaced, on the verge of being forgotten forever as everyone grows up around him.

I wish my neighbors would have the boys meet somewhere else in the mornings or have them play at Joe's house up the street after school to give me a break. The kids would never have to know why, of course, because that would be hurtful, but I feel as though the adults could surely grasp that seeing them so often would be hard on Tim, Margaret, and me.

My best friend, Diana, comes to visit and must navigate her car around the two boys and their go-karts in the driveway to park under the ironwood tree. In the kitchen her eyes grow wide. "How do you do it? Every time I have one of Lucy's friends in my car, I know that if anything happened to that child, through no fault of my own, my friendship with the parents must be sacrificed. It would just be too painful for them to see me or Lucy. But, man! You can't avoid any of it! It kills me, Anna."

It kills me too. I don't want to run away from people and places, from my feelings, and certainly not my grief, but I'm struggling. I'm sure people wonder if we'll move, but who has the energy for something that colossal? We just lost our son! I don't want to have one more loss—the loss of our home, his home.

I talk to my pastor Linda over lunch. "It's hard to feel like crap every time I see my neighbors. I know it's my issue and that I need to change. I should be more loving, but it hurts so much. It feels like if I reach out to them in love, I'll just be faking it, and I'll lose even more. Somehow, it feels like that would mean Jack didn't matter."

She touches my hand. She is a pastor, a mother, and my friend who still cries at night when she thinks of Jack in the creek. She doesn't tell me I should be kinder or holier. "There are no *shoulds* here, Anna. Go easy on yourself. If your hand is raw, it's okay to put a balm on it to protect it. It doesn't negate the injury; it just makes it feel a little better. It soothes it. Finding a balm doesn't mean you are running away from the pain and the grief. Is there a balm you can find in this situation?"

I can't think of one, but the image sticks with me. And I'm starting to realize that seeing the two boys every single day scrapes the edges of my wounds anew.

Halloween is our first holiday without Jack, a day that brings up sweet reminders of him dressed as a panda, a bee, and a pirate. I'll never forget how surprised he was when I brought home one costume that he ended up wearing three years in a row: the Zombie Doctor. He knew I didn't like gore, and said, "I love it, Mom! I really can't believe you bought me this!"

"Me either" was my satisfied reply.

This year, Tim takes Margaret and Alexis around the neighborhood, and the girls shiver in Alice in Wonderland costumes too cute to cover up with coats. It is Margaret's first time trick-or-treating without Jack. He had never ditched her to go off with his friends. I try to be enthusiastic for her sake, decorating the house, buying her costume, choosing which candy to hand out.

When I see Joe and Daniel standing in the driveway outside our kitchen door having their pictures taken in matching costumes, I know I'm screwed. Screwed. I now know there will be no subtle steering to encourage the boys to play somewhere else. There will be no balm. No gentle conversations about the strange but important ways parents need to mourn. Obviously, the parents and grandparents cannot see how painful it is to have Joe and Daniel around so much. Maybe things would be different if I were brave enough to ask for what I need.

When Joe and Daniel knock, I smile numbly and hand them their candy. After waiting a few more minutes, I turn out the front porch light, leaving the candy bowl on our metal glider for whoever else comes by. I just can't do this.

One day, much later, Daniel's grandmother Donna calls me on the carpet, out by my trash can as I try to get in my car.

She has been watching me. "You slam your car door when you get in. You don't smile. You don't say hello anymore. The boys are afraid of you! You don't need to hug them, Anna, but you must say hello!"

Her words leave me feeling stunned and defeated. I feel like a failure as a mother. A neighbor. A human. She's right. I wish I was in a position to make the boys feel better, but what she is asking me seems like far too much.

By that time my relationships with Joe's and Daniel's families feel most likely beyond repair. Somehow, Tim is able to look the parents and grandparents in their eyes as he walks Shadow and say a warm hello and make small talk, even though he tells me that seeing the boys shooting baskets and riding bikes in the driveway hurts him to his core. He has found a way to compartmentalize, but that frustrates me too. When he stops to chat with Joe's father as we attempt a walk around the block, I want to scream, "Our son died right there in his backyard! Why are we all acting like everything is normal?"

I am aware I have grace inside me and it's flowing out with some people and not others. That doesn't feel good. I have an epiphany that Donna and I are both just trying to lessen the pain a bit, her for the boys, me for myself. It's an impossible situation.

I eventually do begin to wave and say hello again. I don't want to, especially because I don't like being told what to do. These small efforts are excruciating and make me miserable. But the opposite choice, to continue to ignore the boys, doesn't feel like who I am either.

And who am I, anyway?

How is it possible that I have gone from the friendly mom who threw Friday night happy hours and s'mores parties in the cul-de-sac to becoming a scary, bitter neighbor lady?

twenty-two

"You did this! You did this!" I yell, my face twisting in pain and rage. I'm at a stoplight, yelling at God. I catch a glance of myself in the rearview mirror. I look ugly and unhinged. If the people in the cars next to me look over and see me alone, gripping the wheel as my mascara pools on my face like two black eyes, would they guess I'm yelling at God?

I tell my friends, just as I used to assure Jack and Margaret, that it's okay to get mad at God. That He can take it. And I've come to find that although many people's faith has been strengthened after Jack's death, I have other friends who are so angry and hurt that they consider it the last straw in their relationship with Him. For the most part, though, I've considered myself more shocked and let down than mad. But usually when we tell our kids, "I'm not mad; I'm disappointed," there's still an underlying current of anger as we grit our teeth and try to sound a lot more mature than we really are. We aren't fooling them, and I guess I'm not fooling God. I'm mad.

On a recent morning, I put my head in my hands at the kitchen table, saying out loud in frustration, "Why would God give us warning signs if He was still going to take Jack? If we couldn't do anything to save him?" I don't mean for Margaret to hear me, but she does. She rounds the corner, "God didn't make it happen, but He *knew* it was going to happen."

Oh. I guess that could explain why He would warn us but not intervene. Maybe He is a God who watches, watches, watches as events unfold, knowing about them in advance. But that makes me see Him as puny and powerless. If my God is powerless, I really have no cause to blame Him, and He gets off the hook pretty easily. If He just set the world in motion and then stepped back and let it go, that's one thing. Shit happens. Sin happens. Floods happen. Accidents happen.

But I don't want an impotent God. I don't want my God to be creator and then mere observer, with some advance warnings thrown in. I want a big God. A God with a plan. A God who is intimately involved in my life right here, right now.

And if my God is a big God with a plan, I hate His plan. Not just for us, but for so many others who suffer in this world. I'm afraid to tell people that I often believe God had a plan for Jack, for us, for them too, because I am afraid God might come off looking cruel and twisted. As mad as I am, I can't seem to slam God. Not because I'm afraid He'll smite me or even be disappointed. He's not a petulant child. He wants me to be real with Him and I will. It's just that deep down I still feel that He can be trusted.

I know I'm not the only one trying on different ideas for size. Liz calls me up and says, "I don't think God caused the accident, but I think He can redeem it," speaking to convince herself as much as me. We do see much that is positive flowing out of our loss, such as moms becoming more accepting of the children God gave them, families realizing that there is more to life than just material things, and people turning toward God for answers and comfort. These are the fruits of our loss, but could they also be a reason for it? Liz doesn't think so.

One idea is that God took Jack. That his days were numbered in God's book from before he was born. That just as God knew Jack intimately, He knew when it was time for Jack to go home to heaven. But He didn't just know this; He made it happen. Because God is in control of everything.

I mean, why are we so ready to give God the credit for every good thing in our lives, from finding our mate, to doing well on a test or landing a job we like, yet we let Him off the hook for all the bad stuff? That seems ridiculous. Isn't He powerful enough to command our destiny? Because that's the God I want to worship, not some good-luck charm we call upon to help us find a parking space when we're running late. I want a powerful God who is willing to make the hard, unpopular choices because He sees the big picture and knows what's best. Sure, He wants our worship, but He doesn't need our approval.

I play with the idea that our son's death is not a random accident, not just the result of free will and bad judgment and freak weather, but somehow part of a larger plan. And a loving God, who holds all the pieces in His hands, can see the plan that we cannot.

Some people point out that perhaps Jack was spared some greater pain and heartache by dying young. His violent death in the creek makes it hard to imagine how this spared him from anything, but I consider this idea too, turning it over in my mind. He was the child I worried most about, because he felt things so intensely. Did the accident spare him some deeper pain? Jack never faced abuse, addiction, or even a broken heart. He never strayed from God. He never had a day without feeling loved and hopeful. He died on a spectacularly fun day. One in which he couldn't quit smiling. But I have a hard time believing that he needed being spared of anything, because Jack was an overcomer, and I wanted him to have a chance to keep overcoming.

Or did Jack die because of something I've done or not done? Was our suffering meant to build perseverance and character in Tim and me? To make us depend more fully on God? Or are those just more fruits of what happened? I can't believe in a God who would take my son in order to make me more compassionate, loving, or holy. I'm afraid that would be a deal breaker.

And then there are the moments I don't tell anyone about, when I feel like a bad griever. When I step into the crisp fall air, the sunshine warms my hair, and laughter comes quickly and easily. A gentle sense of contentment rests on me. Part of my brain feels aware that God is using Jack's shocking death for something important, and that feels powerful and holy and somehow good, even though I don't understand the details.

In these fleeting moments, and on these rare days, I can look beyond our circumstances for a while, away from what Jack is missing out on, away from the creek, and feel joy and hope. I don't know what I'm hoping for, because the thought of a future without Jack makes my stomach turn. But thinking of Jack doesn't. It makes me smile and fills me with gratitude that he was once mine and somehow still is.

These moments give me a break from the pain. I wonder if they are the result of so many people praying for us, taking some of the burden onto themselves. I think of the verse, "The LORD is close to the brokenhearted," and I wonder if that's what I'm feeling, a God so close that my broken heart becomes a broken *open* heart, more like a vessel able to receive love, comfort, and grace that is closer than my own skin.

I try not to analyze this too much. There's no guilt over my lack of tears or the laughter that leaves me shaking my head, remembering something funny that Jack did or said, some little memory of family life. I just accept these moments and call them "pockets of peace." It is a peace that makes little sense in our circumstances. It is a peace that is completely incongruous with a wrenching away, a violent death, dashed dreams, and wasted potential. Is this "the peace...which transcends all understanding?" Whatever you call it, I'm desperate and hurting, and I'll take what I can get.

twenty-three

I 'm surprised in early November when Tim asks me to take a walk with him, because we haven't really gone anywhere alone together since the accident. We park near the bike path, and he leads me far into the woods, so far that I figure he either wants to make out with me or murder me.

Instead, he wants to talk, which is what I want too. But it's so hard. We are not very good at communicating, and we have never felt the need to talk very much, even in the early years of our relationship. I remember how one of my best friends told us she and her fiancé would stay up until the wee hours, grappling with big issues and digging into their feelings together. Tim and I both thought that sounded exhausting. Without a lot of discussion, we tend to agree on the big things and muddle along on the little ones. Sometimes we'll be in the middle of a spat before we realize we are saying the same thing, just expressing it differently.

And now pain hangs in the air between us.

It's time to figure out what we are going to do next. Tim starts, tentatively, "Should we try to have another baby so Margaret won't feel so alone?"

I answer, "I don't know. I just don't know if it's the right thing to do now. We should have tried that a long time ago."

He doesn't say anything. He's trying to look ahead, but I'm bringing up the past, as I tend to do. He starts again. "Should we move out of the neighborhood? It's just so miserable."

I'm relieved that he's bringing up exactly what I've been thinking, but I can barely focus on his words because we're now walking beside a creek. A creek with ragged, jagged edges and sides that go straight down. A creek full of sharp branches, scary twists, and maybe an inch of water at the bottom. The same creek that killed Jack. It's on the other side of the road, the road that flooded that night, but it's the very same creek! Even though there is nothing but sand and an inch of water in the creek, it horrifies me.

How could Tim possibly bring me here? Does he not understand that this would traumatize me? How is *he* not traumatized by it?

As the weeks turn into months after Jack's accident, it becomes even clearer to me that, like our different perspectives of this walk at the creek, Tim's and my grief processes are entirely different from each other. In some ways, Tim's and my preaccident roles have reversed. After a long day at work, I just want to be at home, surrounded by the familiar—the walls smudged with Jack's and Margaret's handprints, the junk drawers filled with bits and pieces of our lives. I want to keep Tim and Margaret close. I want to cocoon and sift through objects that mean something to me. My energy remains low.

But Tim has continued to grow more social and outgoing. He wants to stay busy and connect with people. We don't discuss this change, but it becomes clear in his eagerness to have something to do, to take away the quiet hours. To him, a full square on the family calendar is preferable to another sad, empty day. Guys from the neighborhood and the pastor from the new church in town start getting together once a week to read the Bible and discuss where God is in the midst of what happened to Jack. They bond late into the night over beer and the Bible. It's a welcome chance for Tim to build deeper, more meaningful friendships.

Tim has started asking friends to go hiking and geocaching with him, have a catch in the yard, or watch baseball games on TV. To me that sounds excruciating because those were his special activities with Jack. But in doing them, Tim feels more connected to his boy.

He had just started running in the late summer when friends gave us their old treadmill, and now he begins training for races for the first time in his life: a 5K, a 10K, and before too long there will be marathons. The punishing physical activity gives him a structure to follow and an outlet for his pain. Soon he'll add an adult soccer league and tennis dates to a schedule that already includes our church softball team. When he tells me a dad across town has invited him over to play badminton, I burst out laughing. What's next? Croquet?

One night, he stays out until 2 a.m. making sausage with our neighbor. Sausage.

Margaret begins to notice that Tim is gone a lot and she misses him. She says in her sassy voice, but with an edge of neediness, "What? Is Daddy out with his 'cool new friends' again?" I'm glad to see my girl can still rock the air quotes, even at a time like this, but it's clear she worries we are no longer enough for him, that he is leaving us behind. She wants him home more, but it's hard to justify because all Margaret and I want to do is sit on the couch and watch TV, and that seems like a waste of time to Tim. He doesn't see that sitting next to each other on the couch watching shows about cupcakes or kiddie beauty pageants, while not ideal, is a way for us to bond right now.

If I tried to share my concerns with Tim, he'd get defensive, as if we are trying to deprive him of a much-needed break after he's managed to work all day. But the sad truth is, Margaret's right; we're *not* enough. In the same way, Tim and I are not enough for Margaret, and Margaret and Tim are not enough for me. But how could we be? Every person in a family matters, and when one is gone, the family is off-kilter and lacking.

Tim is doing what it takes to stay alive, and that is an effort I'm relieved he's making. When I get annoyed, I try to remind myself of the alternatives. He could comfort himself alone in the basement or at a bar with a bottle. Or in the arms of another woman. He could be unable to go to work and support us, adding another layer of stress and uncertainty to our precarious situation. He could buy a gun and find a way to be with Jack sooner rather than later. He could get in his car and just keep driving. In our new world, none of these options is beyond imagination, and his busyness and the connections he's forming with new friends seem a lot healthier.

I haven't yet gone back to my old routine of planning our meals for the week as I used to. Sure, I'll cook and we'll eat, but I don't really care what. But

Tim does care; he needs to know there is a plan, so on Sunday afternoons he jots down a week's worth of meals on a Post-it note and starts to cook more. The laundry gets done, the house stays pretty clean, and I manage to take Margaret to the mall a respectable number of times, because that's what tween girls do for fun. I'm even the classroom mother this year, something I signed up for before the accident. But I'm not going to go out of my way to look for something to do. In a way I feel like I'm conserving my energy for some unknown obligation ahead. For a lifetime without Jack.

For the most part, despite small daily irritations and more painful ones like this walk in the woods, we have been loving each other well since the accident, each recognizing the enormous pain of the other. We are a tiny, private club who understand just how much was lost in the creek.

But now I stagger in the woods and begin to cry, wondering how I've ended up with a dead son, a frightened daughter, and a husband who can't even understand why it would be hard for me to be by a creek, any creek, let alone this one. In my heart I cry out to God in despair. I want a sign. I want help. I want to be known.

There's been so much love from our community, from friends and strangers, through all their prayers and the royal-blue ribbons around town. But here, in the woods, I feel desperate and very alone, even with my husband just five feet in front of me on the narrow path. And there, in the middle of the dense woods, hanging down from a branch, is a royal-blue ribbon. Maybe it's from a balloon that flew out of a child's hand and traveled a mile or two before landing. Maybe a bird brought it out here to add to its nest. I reach up to touch it and feel less alone. I don't try to explain my tears to Tim, but say, "I really want to go home now," before I stagger through the underbrush to get back to the car.

Everyone's heard that it's hard for a marriage to survive the loss of a child. I don't know the statistics and am in no rush to find out. Let's just say that even this soon after Jack's death, I'm aware the deathwatch for our marriage has begun.

Do friends and strangers wonder how all this will play out? Perhaps it will be the dramatic plot line of an already weak and fractured marriage being unable to withstand the death of a child. Or the one with a man and a woman who are crazy in love, but the different ways they cope with grief drives them apart.

But what of a rather quiet, ordinary marriage? Of two people who fell in love in college and built a family around faith and fidelity but who in many ways have never made their marriage a priority?

On one hand, I feel more connected to Tim than ever. Our mutual love for our children is enormous.

But what about the years of leaving our marriage mostly untended as we focused on work and kids and church obligations? What about the brittleness, selfishness, and lack of generosity of spirit that crept in as little hurts and resentments piled up over twenty years? And what about the different ways we're coping now?

I can barely force myself to care. I'm too weary and wounded. It's as if I'm observing our relationship from the outside like an anthropological study. The word *cleave*, one of my favorite vocabulary words, pops into my head. It's an unusual word with two opposite meanings: to cling together and to split apart. With the pain, guilt, and grief of losing our son, which definition of *cleave* will describe our marriage?

One thing I know we have going for us is that we don't jump into or out of anything. We used to joke about how some of our friends got divorced and then remarried in less time than it took us to choose a flat-screen TV. Impetuous we are not. Another plus is that we are easily overwhelmed. We never even took the kids to Disney World. It just seemed so daunting and exhausting. I know Disney is doable. People do it every day. But we aren't those people.

So I don't sense a risk that Tim and I will make any rash decisions about our marriage in the midst of our grief, but the old grievances and irritations are still there, topped with the colossal, brutal pain of losing Jack.

twenty-four

Margaret's at a sleepover. It's been almost two months since the accident. We have a small window when there will be two people, not three, in the bed. I know what's coming. We move around the house, satellites orbiting the same planet, but not coming close to each other.

Tim works in the upstairs office, occasionally coming down to the kitchen where I sit, trying to stimulate my fractured brain with a crossword puzzle. I walk to the washing machine to switch a load and can hear he is now somewhere else in the house. If we wait too long, it'll get late. I'll get tired and say no. If I make myself too accessible, it might look as though I'm initiating, which I am not. I try to stay under the radar yet semiaccessible because we're going to have to face this at some point, and maybe that means tonight. We cross paths in the family room where I'm about to turn on the TV.

"Do you want to fool around?" he says, with a look neither hopeful nor horny.

He looks sad.

"Okay," I say, putting down the remote and slowly heading upstairs. My voice is neutral. I'm glad he's asked, because although in the immediate aftermath of the accident the idea of sex was unthinkable, I know it's something we should consider now. We sit upright on the bed, our shoes hanging off the edges, more like acquaintances on a train than spouses.

"Do you think I'm a jerk for wanting to have sex?" he asks.

"No." And I mean it. Why wouldn't he want to do something that can make him feel better and take his mind off reality for a little while?

In general my willingness to have sex is not guaranteed even in the most positive of circumstances. A messy house, stress about the kids, or a long to-do list can throw me off-kilter and derail the whole thing before Tim even knows he's in trouble. He has learned that even if things look favorable, there's no guarantee we'll get to the finish line. And now, with the complication of grief, his proposition is especially risky. Sex brought us our children and will always be linked with them.

He continues in his formal way, "It's just that you don't really want to on a normal day, so I can't imagine you want to do it now." I nod. He gets it. I wish I had been a more fun, spontaneous wife when things had been easier. But I thought life had been difficult then.

I remember reading that sex can be one of the greatest comforts to a man. So I say yes. We make it through. And it is good. I'm proud of us, but I wonder how long it will be before we can do it without both of us crying.

twenty-five

I t's late November. The agent at the airline ticket counter takes our itinerary and IDs and says, out of the blue, "Oh! For some reason I thought there'd be four of you." Tim, Margaret, and I meet eyes, and I say to myself, *So did I, lady...so did I.* Soon we are up above the clouds on our way to LA. We're going to meet Margaret's idol, singer Justin Bieber, thanks to an online campaign by blog readers, friends, and strangers.

It all starts in early October when Tim keeps Margaret home from school on a rough morning. It's clear by the time her classmates are sitting in math class and we are still trying to force her to get herself dressed, that school is not the place for her today. I try to explain that if she needs a day at home, it would be nice to let us know a little earlier, before we are all yelling and crying. It would save so much energy. I head to work and Tim stays home with her. They are less prickly with each other than she and I are. They relax, ride bikes, and run errands.

Margaret makes a wish list of what she wants her errands to yield:

Carrots

Cheerios

Apple Sauce

Pirate's Booty

Black Clay

Bike Helmet

Private Concert with Justin Bieber

Jack!

"Jack" is underlined nine times.

I post the poignant list on my blog. We all want to give her what she needs most, but in the face of this impossibility, thousands of caring people rally around to help her meet her idol. They spread the news and call in favors. If all goes smoothly, Margaret will see Justin rehearse a song for the American Music Awards and then attend the awards show that evening. She might even get to meet him. I'm not sure how I'll be able to handle that, because the slight, brown-eyed superstar looks a little too much like the kid we're missing, just with earrings, tattoos, and some strangely baggy pants.

It's hard to believe we are on our way to meet the biggest music superstar in the country. We're just normal people, or at least we were until September 8. We never sought to rub shoulders with anyone famous. But people want to do something special for us, to reach out in kindness in this new, raw reality. I wonder if other grievers feel it too, how strange it is to somehow be rewarded for tragedy and loss. On the other hand, this is a gift to Margaret. And we are grateful, because if anyone deserves to have some good come her way out of this horrible bad, it's Margaret.

Margaret hasn't been on a plane since she was three, because money issues and life always seemed to get in the way. She's worried about airplane safety, as she is about so many other things right now, and her face flushes red with rising anxiety. "Plane crashes are extremely rare," I tell her as I squeeze her hand. She swallows and looks out the window. I want to say the old adage, "You take more of a risk getting into a car every day than on an airplane," but I stop my-self. I don't want to add cars to the growing list of things that make her wary. After all, we have to get to school somehow.

In truth, I'm wishing airlines weren't so safe. I wouldn't be at all upset if this plane went down somewhere over Kansas or Colorado. I know it's not fair to suck the airline crew and other passengers into my grief, but I would not be heartbroken if somehow just our little row, 14 D–F, could go to heaven today. At least we'd all be together. Such is the heaviness of family life with one man down.

The plane doesn't crash, we land safely, and we try to live in the moment that so many people have made happen for our little girl. I've told Margaret all about the warmth, sunshine, palm trees, and glamour of Hollywood. So of course it's pouring in LA. The streets are flooding and a cold wind blows, as if we somehow bring our own little cloud of doom with us wherever we go. We rally for Margaret, but even the smallest efforts are exhausting.

We don't have to do much anyway, because Margaret finds LA frightening and wants to stay close to the beautiful hotel. "Why are there bars on the windows?" she asks as we drive through the streets with small grocery stores, pawnshops, and children standing under awnings out of the rain. "Well, this part of the city isn't the safest place to grow up. There's a crime problem. You are lucky to have been born in a place where children are safe to play outside and don't have to have bars on their windows."

She double-checks her seat belt in the rental car, and I wonder why I ever thought it was okay that my kids lived in a safe place, when so many kids did not. We live twenty-five minutes from the inner city, but how often did I think of those children, with bars on their windows? Did I think my kids deserved to be safer than other kids? I'm angry at myself and my small heart, and I'm angry that a seedy strip in LA suddenly seems safer to me than a suburban cul-de-sac in Virginia.

The next afternoon, Margaret meets her idol, who speaks to her kindly and graciously and gives her a kiss on the hand. We see him rehearse, which, when you think about it, is the private concert she wished for. The thousands of people who form our online community rejoice in the bit of lightness and hope that Margaret's smile brings.

Later, we put on our fancy clothes and slosh through the cold puddles to the concert hall for the awards show. Margaret is excited and optimistic. She sparkles. We smile and take lots of pictures, showing that we can and will rise to this occasion on her behalf.

The first act comes out and launches into a song called "If I Die Young." Our families and friends watching at home must have let out a collective gasp. I bite the inside of my cheeks, willing myself not to cry as they sing about a mother losing a child and the child asking God to send a rainbow to shine down on her mother.

I listen to the words, still in disbelief that I buried my child. Outside, the torrential wind and rain finally stop and the sky clears. A friend visiting the city snaps a photo of what she sees over the concert hall as we sit inside. A rainbow.

We wave glow sticks and enjoy the music and the questionable costumes of the performers. I can feel the prayers of the people lifting me up. Helping me smile at Margaret. Our community is with us. God is with us. In this moment it somehow feels like Jack is too.

twenty-six

B y late fall I've only been down once to the cross by the side of the road. I'm finally ready to walk there again. It's still hard to believe that Jack's body was found exactly where I knew it would be.

My friend Anne stops by and asks if I want her to go with me. I do. We turn left out of the neighborhood, walk down the sidewalk along the road, and there it is. How many seconds would it have taken me if I had just ditched my car and run that night? I still wonder: *Could I have saved him?*

I touch the cross and take a few pictures with my phone. People have tied blue ribbons on it and placed trinkets on the ground: toy cars, a teddy bear, a pumpkin, a Lego. I take pictures of the creek bed too, almost dry, even though it has rained hard each day this week. It seems grisly and grim to have this kind of picture on my phone right next to the last picture I took of the kids together, doing their homework and eating apples and peanut butter by candlelight, oblivious to what is coming.

I want to share the cross photos with my blog readers, so they'll see that people in our town are taking care of us and finding ways to memorialize Jack. I know they worry. I want them to see that even the busiest drivers must pass this cross and notice that something that matters happened here.

That evening we are headed to church for one of Jack's and Margaret's favorite yearly projects, packing shoeboxes full of toys for children in poverty around the world. Now Tim, Margaret, and I will push through the pain as we lead a group of elementary kids in the project in honor of Jack.

On the way we stop at our local pizza place, brimming with families enjoying a Friday night ritual. Standing in line among the smiling families, I feel hurt and bitter, so I go outside on the porch while Tim and Margaret pick up our food, single slices now, not a whole pizza like before.

I hear music coming from my purse. It's my phone. I use it for Facebook, texting, and to take pictures. I rarely make calls on it, and I never use it to play music, so it's surprising to hear the words of a familiar Christian song burst forth as I scramble to locate it in my messy purse. I've heard the words on the radio many times before, but now it is as if they were written just for me:

There's a cross on the side of the road
Where a mother lost a son
How could she know that the morning he left
Would be the last time—she'd trade with him for a
          little more time
So she could say she loved him one last time
          And hold him tight.
But with life we never know
When we're coming up to the end of the road
So what do we do then
With tragedy around the bend?

I've gone down to the cross today and now my phone starts playing a song, *this song,* on its own? I stand under the bulb of the restaurant's porch light looking at the phone in wonder, when it reaches the chorus,

We live we love
We forgive and never give up
Cuz the days we are given are gifts from above
And today we remember to live and to love.

It's too much for me to think about never giving up at this point. "Never" seems like such a big commitment. Forgive? Do I even need to forgive anyone? God? Myself? The kids who came knocking on our door? Jack?

I don't know what to make of my phone taking on a life of its own again, like it did on the night of the accident when Romans 8:38–39 appeared on the screen. But tonight I do know I can try to live and love, even though it takes more effort and strength than I think I have. Peace fills me as I walk back inside to get Margaret and Tim and consider this strange message that points me toward life.

"Thanks," I say, whether to God or Jack…I don't know.

III

rara avis

twenty-seven

S oon I start to hear about the dreams. One friend sees Jack, beaming in front of a huge plate of hamburgers, which would have burdened him in life, because he was such a slow eater. In the dream he digs in and is able to finish it all, saying, "I'm okay! Have fun!" Others dream of Jack saying, "Tell my mom and dad I'm happy" and "Tell my mom and dad I'm fine." There's a dream of a much-taller Jack, smiling and silent.

I tuck these dreams in my heart, holding them like small scraps of something hopeful, like fleeting glimpses of my son. "How did he look? How did he seem?" I'll ask, as if my friends have run into Jack around town somewhere or on a trip.

My favorite dream comes from my friend Debbie whose daughter Katie died in a car crash four years before Jack's accident. In the dream Katie and Jack are together even though they never met on earth. Debbie looks into Jack's big brown eyes and asks him if there's anything he wants to tell his parents, fully expecting him to say, "Tell them I'm fine." Instead, Jack says, "Tell my mom and dad they took good care of me." For parents who have to fight the guilt that we did not protect Jack from danger, this smooths some of the jagged edges of our broken hearts.

Later, I'll learn that the night before the accident, a friend who lives out of state dreams of Jack, even though she knows him only from our yearly camping trips. She sees Jack and a woman, both wearing white, sitting in a field of black-eyed Susans while Jack builds something with Legos. When Jack dies the next day, she is stunned. It isn't until months later, when she sees a photo of my mother for the first time, that my friend realizes who Jack was with in the dream. I tell her I've associated black-eyed Susans with my mom ever since I was a little girl.

Hearing about this dream affects me in two ways. I love the idea of Jack being with my mother. But I wonder, is this a premonition, along the lines of the forebodings we experienced before the accident? Does God still warn people through dreams as He did in the Bible? Does this mean we could have prevented Jack's death? And if so, why not give *me* the dream instead?

I don't know, but I choose to believe that these dreams are meant by God to bring comfort, not trouble.

Dreams are one thing, but then there are the visions. Betsy, a missionary who's home on a visit from central Asia, has a vision during Jack's memorial service, of Jack and my mother holding hands, walking together.

Cindy, sobbing in her bedroom the night of the accident, sees me standing on a stage, surrounded by bright lights, speaking to hundreds of people. "I don't know why I saw you instead of Jack that night. It wasn't in a church, so I knew it wasn't a memorial service. You were sharing an important message, Anna." We can't know then that on Mother's Day weekend I'll speak to a packed theater about the crisis of identity that comes from losing that which is most precious to any mother.

Then my best friend, Diana, experiences Jack in her room when she wakes up during the night. She sees a form and senses a peaceful presence that disappears once she is able to identify it as Jack.

I don't know what that's like to have a vision. Does it play out inside your head, like a dream, or is it something you see in front of your eyes as if you're watching a movie? I don't have visions, and I barely dream of Jack. Maybe it's because I'm so used to having him with me, anything less than flesh-and-bone Jack screams lack rather than presence.

Or maybe it's because of how I was raised. In all my years of following Christ, visions, dreams, and miracles seemed to be things we talked about only in relation to biblical times, or at the very most, they'll get a quick mention on the very back page of one of my Christian magazines. These short articles inspire me, mystify me, and lead me to see that perhaps God is involved in not just the big things but the small ones too. But it usually stops there, with a quaint, feel-good story.

I'm not prepared when dreams, visions, and other supernatural signs begin to happen in relation to Jack's death.

For example, a blog reader from Mozambique, who is visiting South Africa, rides along a highway with her husband. She is talking about our loss, my blog, Jack. In front of her she sees a pickup truck with Jack's Bible verse, Luke 1:37, painted on its tailgate.

She can't believe what she's seeing and takes a quick picture to send me. When she looks at the photo later, ready to e-mail it, she notices that the bridge they were going under the instant she took the picture had words emblazoned on the side. So with the bridge on top, and the pickup truck below, the image in the photo reads "Start Living a Better Life Now" and "For Nothing Is Impossible with God."

I'm encouraged by her experience, of course. But I also wonder, are we all so overwrought with grief at the thought of a little boy gone too soon that we're seeing things? Wishing? Grasping? Trying to see connection and significance where there is none? Or could it be that at times like this, when the unimportant falls away like chaff to the ground, we are finally able to recognize what God is doing in the world around us every single day?

Can I believe that the Bible verses that appear on my phone and Jack's silhouette on the wall are not just coincidences but are supernatural comfort for me in the exact moment I need them? What about when another image pops up on my phone, an image of Jesus in a white robe walking up a staircase into a bright light with the words "Follow Me"?

"I'm trying," I say when I see it.

Despite feeling scattered and disorganized, I find a legal pad and begin to write down what I experience and what others share with me. The pages fill up quickly.

I don't even know what to title my list. Miracles? Jack sightings? God winks? Comfort? I'm too busy missing Jack and trying to take care of Margaret to make much sense of any of it right away, but I choose to accept any comfort these signs bring. I reassure myself that if I'm losing my mind, a whole bunch of other people are too.

twenty-eight

My hip bones jut through jeans that were once too tight. I realize that losing ten pounds is what I wanted just a few months ago, but now I take no pleasure in it. I continue to get dressed and put on makeup for Margaret's sake. I will not retreat into my own head and forget about my daughter. People say, "I don't know how you get out of bed in the morning." There is only one reason, but I don't want her to know that. That's too much pressure for one little girl.

But just as the extra padding on my body has disappeared since the shock of the accident, there is little cushion left in our mother-daughter relationship. I want to cuddle, to hold her close, but there is a push-pull going on. She keeps me at a distance all day long, occasionally scooching up to sit on my lap after dinner. I am always ready for her when she does this and try to hang on for the ride. But I don't squeeze too hard, knowing that any neediness might push her away. I still don't have many words to pray to God, so I simply add the words *Help us!* to the list in my soul. *Jack is dead. I will not kill myself today. Help us!* No lofty prayers here.

"Grief in a ten-year-old girl looks a lot like anger," the counselor, whom Tim and I start seeing every two weeks, tells us. Margaret holds her shit together all day at school and at soccer. She is charming and witty and brave. Her laugh comes easily. But at home, she lashes out at me in anger and pain, usually over something small, refusing to admit that what she is spewing is really unspoken grief and a profound disappointment with the way her life is turning out.

Margaret criticizes my words, facial expressions, and even my intentions. My mouth opens, then closes again as I come up with something that might be helpful to say to her, then think better of it. It feels like everything we built is now on shifting sand. I am determined to be there for her, but I am fighting for my survival too. It's hard to be her target, but I won't give up.

I don't have a mom like Margaret does, so I dump on my sister, who is also my dearest friend. With her, I am often hopeless, quiet, and angry. I guess I need a safe place to step back from being the grace-filled person who is handling Jack's death so bravely on my blog and with my friends. My heart is bigger and softer than it's ever been, but it's also hurting, and the hurt spills out on Liz.

Liz approaches me gingerly, not knowing whether she'll be met with tears or kindness. She must wonder how someone receiving so much love from all over the world can be so hard on the one loving her best, her sister. Now Liz has lost a mother, nephew, and in many ways, a sister too. It takes me a while to realize I'm treating Liz exactly the same way Margaret treats me.

"Is Margaret seeing a therapist?" is the first question everyone asks. They care. I know I would ask the same question if the roles were reversed. I want to say, "Yes, it's art therapy, and it's awesome!" but I just answer, "We're working on it." What I want to say is, "Back the hell off. I'm trying my best."

The idea of therapy scares Margaret, a problem made worse by our taking her to a trauma therapist on a stormy Thursday night exactly two weeks after the accident. Margaret had fear and betrayal in her eyes as the counselor led her down the long hallway away from us. She refused to say a word. She thinks if we make her go to therapy, we are labeling her as broken or crazy.

I see so much of my younger self in her, the stoic hard worker who doesn't want to lose control. Opening herself up to talk about her grief could sweep her away with the force of her feelings, and she's not willing to take that risk. I get it.

For months I drag her to a counselor once a week to address her anxiety about getting sick and dying, but this push for therapy is poisoning our relationship. Some of the scenes that unfold between when she gets into my car at the school pickup line and when we park several miles away at the counselor's office look more suited to *The Jerry Springer Show* than our lives.

I don't want Margaret to discover the frightening fact that we really can't make her do anything, so I persist. I can't physically carry her into the offices, but I reason, I beg, I argue, I pray aloud. I use a calm voice that just pisses her off more.

One afternoon, despite my best efforts not to, I start to cry quietly in the front seat. "You are so weak!" she yells at me, disgusted. I think of the strength it has taken to make it to this point in my day. I wonder if someday when she is a mother herself, the weight of my reality will hit her and I won't seem so weak anymore. I hope not. I hope she won't remember these horrible afternoons at all. She's just a little girl trying to survive unbelievable circumstances.

In order to save our relationship, I want to quit forcing her to go to therapy. My gut tells me it's far too soon for her to process her feelings. My gut tells me the struggle outweighs the benefit right now, especially when she sits on the counselor's couch not saying a word. My gut reminds me of the way I processed my mother's death, inwardly, slowly, and on my own timetable. But I doubt my gut now. I doubt myself as a parent.

Eventually, I tell her we can stop therapy for a while, but that she must attend a weekend grief camp in March. The camp counselors tell us to do whatever it takes to get her there, because the camp really is that good. I slip a crisp one-hundred-dollar bill under a magnet on the fridge. "This is yours when you get back from camp," I tell her. She does not agree to go.

But she says, "They'd better not try to pretend it's a normal camp, 'cause it's not." She's right. None of this feels normal, so why pretend?

Margaret also seems to have the same instinct to try to make sense of the world that I had as a child. One day on the way home from school, she asks, "Mom, did you have a good childhood?"

"Yes. It was wonderful," I replied. "Why?"

"Because you're having a pretty bad adulthood."

She continues, "I'm having a pretty bad childhood, but I hope that means I'll have a pretty good adulthood."

Oh, sweetie, me too.

twenty-nine

When Jack was a year old, he and I met Diana for lunch in Fredericksburg. It was one of those Italian places where you doodle on a white paper tablecloth with crayons. As we were leaving, a blue crayon Jack was holding snapped in half. His cries were inconsolable. Sensitive souls that we were, Diana and I hugged him, laughed, and snapped a picture as he wailed.

That pained little face would become familiar to me. It didn't spring up when I would tell him no, because Jack seemed to understand the whys behind right and wrong even so very young. I felt like I could reason with him and that he understood me too. But his abject sadness popped up at unusual times.

Like many preschoolers, Jack and his cousin Isaac were obsessed with wooden Thomas the Tank Engine trains. One day Liz and her kids came for a visit. Trying to seal her most favored aunt status with two-year-old Jack, Liz bought two little train cars that went together—Annie and Clarabel. She thought it would be sweet if Jack had one in Virginia and Isaac had the other in Indiana where they lived at the time—two best-buddy trains for two best-buddy cousins. Jack knew they went together. You know, like peanut butter and jelly or Adam and Eve. Instead of the delight she thought she would see on Jack's face, Liz was greeted with hysterical wailing because she had broken up "the set." Jack was heartbroken that Annie and Clarabel wouldn't be together in the same house. It's not that he wanted both; he would rather have neither if it meant they'd be separated. His brand-new train disappeared into my underwear drawer to avoid causing any more anguish.

Another time, Jack and Margaret, in an attempt to keep themselves entertained during an intolerably long, rainy day at home, climbed up on our wingback chair to look out the picture window of our tiny house. They watched rainwater run down the street and into the gutters. A trash can tipped over, its lid floating in a rush of water down into the sewer below. You would have thought someone had killed a puppy, so sad was Jack's reaction to the plastic lid being swept away from the can.

He was also a stickler for rules, and cheating or lying of any kind sent him into a tailspin. He could suck the fun out of a birthday party activity with lightning speed if someone broke a rule. Jack and Isaac loved *Calvin and Hobbes,* so one year Liz decided the kids would play a round of "Calvin Ball" at Isaac's birthday party. The premise of Calvin Ball is that you get to make up the rules as you go along. What a nightmare for Jack. I spent the party trying to staunch the wailing.

One afternoon, when Jack was in first grade, he approached me in our upstairs hallway, his school uniform shirt smudged with peanut butter, a serious look on his face. "Mom, I want to talk to you about my symmetry," he said, although it sounded more like "symmetwee" in his little-boy voice.

I was surprised he even knew that word. "What do you mean?" I asked.

"Symmetwee. You know, how everything has to be in twos. If I touch something with my left hand, I have to do it with my right. I have to even it up. I need to be symmetwical all the time, and sometimes I get stuck. I don't like it."

So much made sense in a flash. Jack was dealing with obsessive compulsive disorder, which he had aptly named "symmetry." When our doctor asked what the voice in his head said to him when he felt compelled to balance things out, Jack waited a moment, then whispered, "Double it." It sounded relentless. Bossy. Scary. My heart sank to think of him being pushed around by a stupid voice telling him to double his every move.

The fidgeting, the squirrelly walks down the hall touching things or hopping from tile to tile, which looked like goofing off? OCD. The abject sadness when something broke or whenever a set was broken up? The trains Annie and Clarabel? It made sense now. The difficulty he had walking away from a task in school before it was completely finished to his satisfaction? Oh my goodness.

Turns out that OCD runs in my family, and Jack probably always had it, or it may have been triggered by his frequent strep infections. I felt terrible for being angry and frustrated with him. For wanting him to be more laid back. For not always accepting him for who he was.

Jack was matter of fact about his OCD and didn't lament the extra burden he lived with every day. He learned how to use cognitive behavior therapy to strengthen his resistance to the compulsions, and we checked in with a doctor every year or so after that to see how things were going.

Jack worked around the inner buzzing to excel at school. He still made choices that annoyed his teachers, and he spent some time bonding with the principal, but he didn't want special treatment or to be singled out in any way. Besides, sometimes it was hard to decide which antics were part of Jack's fun personality and what was OCD.

Over time Jack became more socially aware, learning to put his inner compulsions aside when possible so that he would fit in with others. On one hand, we wanted the world to be gentle on Jack because of his struggles; on the other hand, we wanted him to learn to function in the world.

And he did. Jack was the adorable, creative, funny kid who made great friends and brought others into his world with made-up games. There were hard times, for sure. I learned early on what most parents of sensitive, quirky kids know: recess and lunch are the worst.

But Jack's OCD, while it helped explain some of his struggles, did not define him. In fact, we forgot to tell Margaret about it, even though they were so close. At first she seemed too young, at age four, to grasp what her brother called "symmetwee." Then it became just another facet of family life. When she was around eight, I casually commented on something Jack was doing. "Oh, that's just Jack's symmetry." She wanted to know what on earth I was talking about. I explained the basics, then gave her a children's book about OCD. "Mom," she said, "you should have told me sooner so I could have been nicer when Jack acted weird."

When I look at Jack's life, both his amazing gifts and his struggles, I am proud of how he handled both success and adversity. I was always learning from Jack.

But when I think of that adorable two-year-old who could never bear to break up a set, I cry. Not because of the OCD, but because it's clear to me that his death broke up something that belonged together, our family. It's still so difficult to believe he's gone.

Clarabel the train was never as far away as Jack thought; he assumed I'd sent it back to Indiana to be with his cousin Isaac, when, really, it was in my dresser drawer the whole time. Maybe Jack is not as far away as he seems either. He'll always be part of this set: Tim, Anna, Jack, and Margaret.

It's tempting when children die to turn them into little saints, because their beautiful qualities shine so brightly in our memories through the lens of our intense longing. In downplaying their humanity, however, we can sometimes deprive them of their full personhood.

I know I run this risk when writing and talking about Jack, so I make sure I talk about his struggles with OCD, his squirrelly behavior in school, and his fondness for the word *butt*. I tell you he got frustrated easily. I want you to know he became so crabby each winter that in second grade I finally had him start sitting in front of a "happy light" January through March. And don't even get me started on how unenjoyable it was to help him write an essay. I want everyone to know that Jack was a real flesh-and-blood boy, not some two-dimensional paragon.

But then I wonder how to share some of the ways in which he was special, because while I don't want to leave the impression I'm trying to build him up into something he wasn't, I also don't want to withhold the amazing ways that Jack was Jack.

Like the way he wrote words ending in *ing* on tiny slips of paper and offered to sell them to his classmates for a penny apiece. How could our son invent something as funny and creative as what he called "Pocket Gerunds" and not have me tell you about it?

Then there are the many moments that show a depth of understanding that surprised us. Like the day six-year-old Jack walked up to my desk, his eyes teary, a sad expression on his face. What was going on? Had someone been making fun of him at school?

"Hey, guy, what's up?" I asked.

"I wish people wouldn't choose transitory joy over what's important," he said.

Huh? What did a little kid know about transitory joy? What did I even know about it? And why on earth was it getting him down?

Turns out his class had memorized this poem:

The Flies and the Honey Pot
by Aesop

A jar of honey chanced to spill
Its contents on the windowsill
In many a viscous pool and rill.

The flies, attracted by the sweet,
Began so greedily to eat,
They smeared their fragile wings and feet.

With many a twitch and pull in vain
They gasped to get away again,
And died in aromatic pain.

Moral:
O foolish creatures that destroy
Themselves for transitory joy.

And while Jack's classmates were enjoying acting out the hand motions of the icky stickiness and the doomed flies' futile attempts to escape, he was pondering why people make the choices they do.

Jack was a patient person, not typically given to excess in his desires or appetites. After eating one or two pieces of his Halloween candy, he'd stash the rest in his room, untouched, until I either ate it or threw it away. He saved up his money for "something big." He didn't sneak around trying to do things that were off-limits.

So I guess I could see how he could be upset at the thought of people focusing on instant gratification or fleeting joys. Jack had never been wired that way. But his statement seemed so mature for a child, because isn't childhood primarily made up of transitory joys?

It was surprising that even at six years old, Jack understood that people are easily ensnared by what appears to be sweet but is in truth harmful.

Looking back now, I wonder if Jack knew something that we didn't—that his life here would be fleeting yet would somehow point others toward things that last?

thirty

I used to be fairly unsympathetic with grievers, at least on the inside. This could have been because I'd lost my mom so early and realized that since grief was going to come to everyone in time, people should just learn to deal with it.

Maybe I was afraid that exposing someone's pain to the light by acknowledging it would somehow make it worse. That it would cause them to dwell on it rather than live life. Maybe I thought they would then want too much from me. Or it could be that I was just woefully bad at math.

See, deep down I thought, *What's one miscarriage when you have two healthy kids?* or *You're falling apart about your divorce, but you brought three beautiful children into the world and you have your whole family behind you.* Or, *You're going on and on about missing your mother, but she was eighty. Mine was forty-six! Think about those thirty-four extra years.*

Of course I never said any of these things out loud. I guess I just didn't get that you can't apply math to grief. Loss is loss is loss. Of course I realize I have a healthy daughter and husband. I love them deeply. But the balance of the two here cannot negate the loss of the one "there."

Stupid math.

thirty-one

C hristmas is here. We keep all our traditions the same for Margaret's sake. I think of last Christmas, when the kids heard there would be a Nativity play at our church on Christmas Eve. Since they both loved to act, they immediately agreed to participate when Tim wanted to sign them up. After a few practices they were less enthusiastic. Kids as young as four were in the play, so at fourth and sixth grades, Margaret and Jack felt overqualified and far too old. "Mom, the girl next to me rubbed boogers in the carpet!" Jack said with disgust. I did not point out to him the preschool concert where he'd spent an entire song digging in his own nose, captured on video by all the parents.

Margaret had a speaking part as a star in the Bethlehem sky. Jack was Joseph, poor put-upon Joseph, in a nonspeaking role, of course. "Mary acts like she's my real wife because she's always bossing me around. I *know* where I'm supposed to stand," he said, perturbed.

Tim and I talked to them about following through on a commitment, and we acknowledged that this particular play was probably not the best fit for them. By the time we went out for our Christmas Eve Mexican lunch right before the play, we were able to laugh about it, boogers and all.

After the service, in which everyone, including the twinkling star and the overqualified Joseph, did an excellent job, Jack came up to me, having peeled off his costume as soon as the organ played the final note. He handed over the wad of tan fabric with flourish and said, "Here, Mom. I'm glad the worst day of my life is over with!" I squeezed his surly sixth-grade-boy shoulders and laughed, saying, "I hope you're right, Jack. I hope you're right."

This Christmas Eve morning, Tim is struggling. He remembers the time Jack suggested we all run around the block and do one hundred jumping jacks to help us fall asleep more easily on Christmas Eve. He remembers staying up late writing rhyming clues for the kids to find where their final present was hidden, and the time the clues led us all down to the mailbox in our Christmas pajamas. He remembers watching *It's a Wonderful Life* snuggled on the basement couch and the kids asking why I always wept when George Bailey is called "the richest man in town."

After a good cry up in his office, Tim asks God for a sign, anything, to comfort him as he faces Christmas without Jack. He comes downstairs to make his coffee and pulls out a crossword puzzle from his work bag, where he has several old newspapers stashed for when he has downtime. This one is from Valentine's Day, February 14, 2011. He sits at the kitchen table and reaches for a pen. (Are we the only ones who do crossword puzzles in ink?) He reads the clue for 1-Across: "Trunk Tool." J-A-C-K.

Thank You.

Christmas morning we go through the motions. We videotape the poem scavenger hunt as usual and tell ourselves, *We can do this. We can do this.* We laugh a lot, make little piles of our presents, and spend the day in our pj's.

But going to the cemetery hangs over us. It seems selfish to stay away, as if we don't care about Jack on this important family day. But the cemetery makes me angry. Jack does not belong there! And through all the signs, I'm finally starting to understand that Jack might be closer to me right here than he is in a cemetery. I find myself getting angry with Tim, because he thinks we should go, but Margaret and I don't want to. Tim must feel lonely and outnumbered.

We put it off until it's almost dusk. As we head out, we drive over the spot where Jack was found. I see a small live Christmas tree there, powered by solar lights. Someone has decorated it and placed wrapped gifts underneath, for Jack's first Christmas in heaven. I want to stop, but Tim knows if we do, it'll be too dark to go to the cemetery. We are like two bratty children, and Margaret, alone in the backseat, yells, "Why are we doing this, anyway?" More fighting means more stress for her. Will I need to stay up with her again tonight, holding her hand as her face flushes with anxiety, she grows hot, and she thinks she'll throw up?

Tim misses a turn and parks on the wrong side of the cemetery. We have to climb down a steep hill and walk through the entire place to get to where Jack's ashes are buried, marked by nothing more than the small plastic marker from the funeral home. Margaret bitches. I bitch. Tim lets out a loud groan of frustration.

We stand there for a moment, seething next to Jack's and my mother's graves. "Let's go." Tim carries Margaret back up the hill on his back. I stomp the cold, hard ground as I walk back to the car. It's too dark now to stop near the creek and see the little Christmas tree. Later, I'll find Hot Wheels cars, Yankees ornaments, and yarn crosses there and will know that Jack must be part of a lot of Christmases this year.

As we pull into our driveway, Daniel's grandmother Donna stands by the trash cans, taking out her Christmas garbage, mounds of festive paper from a big celebration of aunts, uncles, cousins, and grandchildren. Other Christmases we would have spent time with them. But we do not want to see anyone right now, especially someone so entangled with our pain. "Tim, Anna…," she starts, trying to offer us condolences and connect with us as we climb out of the car.

"This is not a good time, Donna!" Tim says roughly, as Margaret and I look away, pressing our faces to the kitchen door, tears on our cheeks, willing him to hurry and unlock the house. We know we're not behaving graciously, turning our back on a friend, but we are past the limit of what we can handle today.

Merry Effing Christmas.

thirty-two

One Saturday afternoon in early 2012, Tim tells me he has decided to take Margaret to the movies. I say that maybe I'll come along, but Tim responds with, "Well, if you can take her, maybe I'll just stay home and get some work done." I'm hurt. I'm not just trying to get childcare coverage for Margaret; I'm trying to get us all to do something together, as a family of three.

Of course Tim would rather stay home and work. So would I. Neither of us is all that interested in seeing the animated movie Margaret has picked. Having someone stay home would be cheaper and more productive; it's true. It would also be less painful. When the three of us are together, Jack's absence is all the more glaring because we can't just pretend that we're tag teaming—with one of us somewhere with one kid, and one with the other—as we have done so many times before.

It doesn't feel right, but this is the family we have now, and I want us to feel it, to try to figure some way to make it work. To go to the movies. To watch TV together on the couch instead of going off into separate rooms. To sit in a restaurant booth and pick which bench will be for one and which for two. To go places without friends and relatives serving as a buffer. Tim and Margaret end up going to the movies by themselves.

A few weeks later, Tim proposes a ski trip that includes grandparents, aunts, uncles, and cousins on his side of the family. Making plans for the future is progress, but it doesn't feel like progress to me. This trip includes flying on an airplane, missing school, spending money, and most likely soaking in a hot tub, which Margaret will love. But for more than a decade, Tim and the men in his family went on big ski trips out west for a week at a time without spouses or kids. They talked about bringing families along someday but always pushed the idea off for later. I resented Tim spending the time and money on those trips at the expense of doing something significant with the four of us.

I give Tim my blessing for this new trip, but I don't really mean it. All I can think of is what a good skier Jack was and how much he would have enjoyed a trip like this. Before, I resented that Tim did not include our family on these vacations, and now I resent that he does.

We must find ways to live life moving forward, but it's excruciating and complicated. At first the idea of doing anything at all seems sickening and deplorable. How could we ever enjoy a single thing again? But we must. There are always holidays looming, birthdays, and vacation time, and there must be a way to navigate them without those who are gone.

I remember driving through town with my mother when I was Margaret's age. We passed a house with a big construction project going on. Out front was a car with personalized plates that read POOR AL. I asked Mom what she thought it meant.

She answered, "I know them. The husband died and they used the insurance money to buy a new car and fix up the house like they'd always wanted. It says 'Poor Al' because Al isn't around to enjoy any of it." I knew the license plates were supposed to be funny, but it sounded more than a little disloyal to me that this family was going on, making improvements, and enjoying life without Al.

That's one of the reasons I had such a hard time accepting the changes I saw in my father after my mother died and he remarried. He was free to grow and thrive in a way we hadn't seen before, enjoying many new experiences, but Mom died while she was still in the busy trenches of family life. It felt like a real "Poor Al" situation to me.

No wonder my feelings are all tangled up when it comes to deciding what to do without Jack. During his childhood, we pinched every penny and rarely splurged on anything, even though we had the money. This simple lifestyle suited us in many ways, but I know we missed opportunities to make even more memories with our family while it was intact. Now we realize that life is short and we should make the most of it, but when we consider doing it without Jack, it devastates me and feels disloyal.

"Poor Al" or "Poor Jack" thinking leads me into regret. I try not to let regrets overtake me, but they are hard to shake. I regret some of the things I did and other things I left undone. I'm sure Tim has regrets too, so I try not to resent him for wanting to do better now that he knows better.

Refusing to at least try to enjoy life out of loyalty for someone who is gone cuts us off from even the chance of good days ahead. It squanders the lessons we've learned about making the most of life now. It compounds the wreckage and devastation. I get that. I really do. But it's all a weird dance, and it's going to take us a while to figure out our steps.

thirty-three

My friend Arian, who had known Jack since he was a baby, tells me that she starts several times to write us a condolence letter but can't seem to make herself do it. Finally, she writes a poem in honor of Jack's first word—an event she clearly remembers—and titles it *"Rara Avis,"* Latin for "Rare Bird."

"I'm not a poet, Anna, but I just knew I had to write a poem," she says. She captures Jack beautifully, and it makes me miss him even more as I allow myself to remember the stages she describes.

Rara Avis
for Jack
by Arian Hadley

"Bird," he signed,
Pudgy fingers fluttering.
We marvel and clap.

"Bird," he spoke,
"Starts with *B.*" So smart, so young.
We wonder and smile.

"Bird!" he yelled.
Too loud for the classroom rules.
We correct and sigh.

"Bird," he imagined,
In stories, games, and colored bricks.
We admire and dream.

"Bird," he joked,
With apt and joyful humor.
We recall and laugh.

"Bird!" he declaimed,
Confident upon the stage.
We bravo and beam.

"Bird," he became.
Why must he fly home so soon?
We call out and grieve.

"Bird," we weep,
"Come back here! You've flown too high.
We cannot see you!"

"bird," he whispers,
"Let my wings enfold your heart.
We will meet again."

It's stunning. I post the poem on my blog to give another glimpse of Jack. Before long, from as far away as Israel and Okinawa, bird stories will pour in from my readers, adding to the list of wonders on my legal pad. They are amazing stories of birds catching people's attention at precisely the moment they think of Jack.

The stories will remind me of a hard, hard night five weeks after the accident when Tim and Margaret were out and pouring rain had managed to cut out our electricity again. And it was 6 p.m. On a Thursday. I sat alone on the living room couch in the dark, wondering if someone could actually die from a broken heart. Then a bird started singing, so close to my ear that it sounded as if it were inside the house. The loudest bird I'd ever heard kept me company

for hours, soothing my soul despite the darkness and pouring rain, until Tim
and Margaret got home. The next morning I found it sitting in a flower pot on
our screened porch, and I opened the door for it and gently urged it back outside. I will wonder what all these bird stories mean.

But first, my college friend Courtney e-mails me. Courtney was two years
ahead of me in school. When I returned to college after Mom died, Courtney
cooked dinner for me off campus, mothering me in small ways I needed. We
became even closer through our sorority Bible study as we explored how to live
out our faith.

After college we lost touch for many years until Facebook came on the scene.
She was one of the first friends I looked up. On her profile, I saw the same beautiful face from twenty years earlier. Farther down the page, Courtney's job was
listed as "An Intuitive." Huh? I thought she taught math. That seemed weird.
And besides, isn't *intuitive* an adjective, like a trait you have, not something you
do for a living? Was Courtney saying she was psychic?

I've never known what people were talking about when they spoke of energy or auras or crystals, and I have lived more than forty years without ever
going near palm readers or tarot cards. Angels had no place in my life either,
except in Bible stories.

I debated whether to send Courtney a friend request. What could we possibly have in common? Would I be supporting something un-Christian or
creepy by "friending" her? After a few days I was like, *Get a grip, woman! It's
Facebook.* So I sent the request. I didn't want to squander a chance to reconnect
with a dear friend just because her job seemed odd to me.

She accepted my request, and we sent each other a few messages about our
families and mutual friends from college days. It was as if no time had passed
at all.

After Jack's death, like many of my college friends, Courtney sends flowers
and encouraging messages. She even comes to his funeral, but we don't get a
chance to talk among the throngs of people.

Her latest e-mail reads: "…I saw your blog about the 'Rare Bird' today. And I just know, Anna, that Jack is sending you a message through me. Sometimes God uses people, as well as iPhone apps. :) Jack is sending love, Anna. So much love."

Jack is sending a message! This idea unnerves and confuses me. Mainly because I've tried so hard to do Christianity "right" all these years. How can I reconcile the Bible's warnings about soothsayers and fortune-tellers with a message from beyond the grave? Then again, how do you explain the way God often uses prophets, signs, visions, and dreams in that same Bible?

I realize that even though I've been following God for decades, I'm woefully uninformed about matters of the spirit. I go around and around. Why is what Courtney has to say somehow different from what my friend the missionary and others have been telling us? Or what my best friend experienced when Jack came to her in her bedroom?

I stress and worry. What if talking to Courtney shakes or even robs me of my faith? I simply can't lose God over Jack's death. God is the one who gives me hope of heaven and even a hint that there could be a purpose in this madness. If I lose Him, what will I have left?

If I listen to Courtney, will I be cheating on Jesus?

Or what if Courtney tells me something so painful and terrifying I can't handle it? What if Jack's soul is tormented by the violent circumstances of his death? What if he doesn't think I tried hard enough to save him? I'm terrified of what I might hear.

I call Liz with my fears. She quickly puts the "cheating on Jesus" question to rest. "Sometimes God uses people who are different to get our attention. Like the three wise men. They were foreigners who studied stars, but they're the ones God led to Jesus. The people who'd been waiting all that time weren't looking for a baby. The wise men had the eyes to see what God was showing them. Maybe God put Courtney in your life because He knows she will get the message to you. Maybe she can help you in a way that you need."

This makes sense to me. God knows that seeking out a psychic is too far outside my comfort zone. Why not reach me through someone like Courtney, someone I already know and trust?

I also wonder if God has been preparing me to hear what Courtney might share. The Bible verse and the premonition given to Margaret over the summer? The miraculous signs in our home the night of Jack's accident? The Holy Spirit filling me with very specific words to speak to both the police and at Jack's funeral, as well as the detailed visions and dreams shared by friends in the days after Jack's death?

Maybe all these things were slowly opening up my very traditional, ordinary heart to be able to listen to yet another example of God's ways not being my ways.

I reflect on more words Tim and I read to Jack at his sixth-grade dinner, *"...we hope you will continue to share with us what is going on in your life, and if we don't understand at first, that you won't give up on us."* Maybe Jack does have something to tell us. Maybe we need to be hit over the head and are going to keep getting signs and assurances until the comfort they offer sinks in.

In the meantime I begin to read everything I can on grief, death, near-death experiences, and heaven. I think we can learn from people who have been privy to sacred glimpses, through near-death experiences, of what comes after life on earth.

Most of these stories have striking similarities, and they make me look forward to heaven more than before. There's a brilliant light and intense feelings of acceptance, well-being, and love. There are loving beings there: angels, deceased relatives, and God. There's often a review of one's life, which is like watching a movie, indescribably beautiful music, and intense periods of learning, work, and understanding many of the mysteries of life. Heaven doesn't sound boring, as Jack and I had feared.

My favorite aspect of near-death experiences is that many people who have them don't want to come back. I want Jack to be experiencing something so wonder-filled and perfect that the loving life we shared here is a flimsy imitation by comparison.

But the aspect of near-death experiences that upsets me is that so *many* people have been saved from the brink of dying and even well over the brink. I want to scream, "Why not Jack?" Surely he could have used a near-death experience for the good of the world! Jack was understanding and articulate. Telegenic, even. I like to write and am not too afraid to give speeches.

If Jack survived, we could have shared his heavenly experiences with our friends, neighbors, and the world. We could cowrite a book. He could start his own blog, *When Jack Came Back*. People would be blessed by his glimpse of heaven, their faith would be strengthened, and I'd still have my son here with me. Wouldn't that be a good way for God to demonstrate His power and care and love? Wouldn't that be better than a broken body and death?

Then there's the guilt of reading about people who survived or were brought back to life after being underwater for a long time. Ten minutes, fifteen, forty-five! On the positive side, they write that they did not feel fear or panic even as their bodies struggled. On the other hand, what if I gave up too easily when I saw the raging water? What if when I immediately felt that Jack's soul was gone, he was just on a temporary trip to heaven and we could have brought him back like so many others?

From digging into the Bible and reading about near-death experiences, I get comfort knowing more about what Jack's experience is like in heaven. But as more days pass, earth is really starting to feel like hell without him.

I finally e-mail Courtney and tell her I'm ready to hear what she has to say. She e-mails me back:

> Well, Anna, since the night Jack died and I heard about the accident on the news, I've been sensing him. Before I even knew he was your son....

Every time I'd see this blue jay, I'd feel it was a message of Jack. I kept
getting the sense that a blue jay is such a "rare bird." And I was curious,
because they aren't rare. When I saw the poem "Rare Bird," about Jack,
I just knew, Anna. Jack is sending you a message through me. Jack is
sending love, Anna. So much love. I'd be happy to share more with you
about this, if or when you are interested. I've helped other parents
before. I never know what message will be there, or even if there will be
one. I also understand if this is not of interest…

I ask her to tell me more, via Facebook, and she says she is able to "experience Jack." Huh? She had not felt led to share this with me over the past weeks
until the mention of "rare bird" popped up on my blog.

"Until I knew the time was right, Anna, I figured whatever I was experiencing of Jack was for my benefit. But now I know it's time to share."

My first, tentative question for her is, "Is Jack okay?" That might sound like
a stupid question when I am 100 percent sure he's in heaven with God. How
much more "okay" can you be? But I think of mothers everywhere, whose children have taken a tumble or had a near miss that could have ended in tragedy.
Even with their child right there, alive and well, moms will hold their babies at
arm's length for a moment to get a better look. "Are you really okay? Are you sure
you're okay?" One hundred times is not too much. I want to hear it again.

Courtney writes back,

Jack is sooooooo far beyond okay! He is exuberant! Like he is busting
out of his mind saying, "This is so cool!" He is loving it! And loving
you so very much! He is happy. Wildly so. His spirit is sooooo beautiful, Anna. I'm moved and awed and humbled to meet him. Often, I
physically feel a soul—emotions—personality. And I feel Jack. He is so
very, very okay. I don't think he suffered at all, Anna. My understanding from what I'm feeling from him is that his spirit left his body before
his body died. That he was not scared. He wanted you to know that.

He shows me that he was immediately helped. He was disoriented and saw people looking for him and was saying, "I'm right here…," but he wasn't in the water. Even by the time you were there, Anna, his spirit wasn't in the water. He was fine. He so wants you to know he is in wonderland. Heaven is nothing like he imagined. Better.

He can be in more than one place at a time. He is giving me an impression of being scooped up…or something like that. It was time. There were beings there waiting to greet him. He was not alone. He was not scared. He wants you to know he was not scared. YOU don't need to be scared.

"Thank you for being my mom." He is expressing so much gratitude in a cuddly blanket kind of way. "You will always be my mom. I don't live in the sky. Why does everyone look up? I'm not up. I'm here (pointing to your heart)." He does NOT mean as a memory. He means alive in your heart.

He is showing me a picture of seeing you look out a window. You don't feel good inside or outside the house. He is helping you. He is saying, "I'm there." He is showing me a picture of Tim throwing a ball in the air and catching it himself. Feels like he is encouraging it. I get the sense of his teasing Margaret, playfully, like "she can have dibs on my room, dude." Enjoy it. It's not a shrine.

He is laughing playfully. Anna, Jack is really an amazing guy. Very bright. Very bright. A rare bird indeed. I love him. He is so gentle for someone with such intense emotional energy. So sorry for your pain, and I'm joining Jack in sending peace and the message that life doesn't end when the body does, though we still miss the body so much.

Courtney goes on to say Jack is not alone but surrounded by others, a group of a dozen or so children, with a special purpose to show that life on earth is not the end. Jack says, "It's really easy here." And again, "It's nothing like I ever expected; it's better."

This is just a snippet of what Courtney has to tell me. For me, her most important words from Jack are that he was not scared and did not suffer. I believe them in my heart instantly. In fact, I think I may have known them all along, even when they were yet unspoken, because I've been relatively free of rumination about Jack being trapped under the water. How is it possible not to be tormented, because he is my heart and his pain is my pain? I believe that peace came from nowhere else but God, and now I get to hear it from Jack.

A few weeks later, Courtney and I get together at her house. We sit, drinking tea and talking. Two old friends. Two mothers. I pray the entire time that our conversation won't do anything to undermine my relationship with God. At the end of our time together, she tells me the most mind-blowing thing: "Anna, when we were talking about Margaret walking toward your car that day, away from Joe's backyard, I saw something as we spoke. It was angels, Anna, flanking her, walking her up the hill and down the street toward you. Margaret couldn't have stayed if she tried. They were getting her out of there. And now I understand why I felt Jack's soul getting 'scooped up' out of the water. It was angels. I know it doesn't make much sense with Jack dying, Anna, but angels have got your babies covered. I just know it."

After I hug Courtney and leave her house, I slide behind the wheel of my car and say, "Amen," ending the silent prayer I've been uttering since I got there. The prayer that I would not dishonor God in any way. I lean over to check my phone for messages.

There, instead of my login screen, are the Bible verses, Romans 8:38–39 (ESV), that appeared there on the night of Jack's accident. I'm starting to think it's time to memorize them: *"For I am sure that neither death nor life, nor angels nor rulers, nor things present nor things to come, nor powers, nor height nor depth, nor anything else in all creation, will be able to separate us from the love of God in Christ Jesus our Lord."*

Nothing. Nothing. Nothing.

This verse has comforted me knowing that death did not separate Jack from God's love even for an instant. Not while slipping, sailing through the air, or while trapped underwater. Now I hold the same words close for myself, knowing that nothing—not my son's death, and certainly not listening to a psychic—can separate this hurting mom from God's love.

In time I will come to consider God the architect of every piece of my interactions with Courtney. God prepared me to hear her, holding her off until I was ready, even though she felt connected to Jack from the night of the accident.

As I read more books and also a letter from a blog reader who nearly drowned twice, I also see how Courtney's summation of Jack's experience of death is similar to the experience of others. Many times even as the body suffers, the soul is already free of the body.

I think about how much comfort this one point can bring to grieving people. I want to spread that peace to all those who love our son, but also to those who worry about their own loved one's final seconds. How gracious God is to people as they transition from life to death!

Still, I'm conflicted about sharing my interactions with Courtney or the other signs with friends, loved ones, and readers.

First, I don't want to make it seem as if Jack is any more special than anyone else. I mean, of course *I* think he is because I'm his mom, but if you knew Jack and his humble personality, you would understand what I mean. When Santa asked him if he'd been good, three-year-old Jack responded, "A little bit." When interviewed for a baseball program about which famous person he would like to meet, he responded, "No one. That would be awkward." Jack was not a guy who asked for special attention or treatment.

And what about people who have lost loved ones but don't get any signs? That's how it has been with my mom, and the last thing I want to do is add to anyone's pain as they grieve.

Second, I'm worried about what people will think of me. Will people think I'm weird if I talk miracles and mystery? When it comes to my blog, I'm pretty sure my words will sound too Christian for some and not Christian enough for others. What if I don't say "Jesus" enough? What if it sounds as though I'm trying to shove God and heaven down people's throats?

Everyone will lose in this world, and signs of comfort remind us that there is great love even in our darkest moments. They don't show me that God is any different from who He says He is, but maybe that He's different from the box I put Him in. Maybe with my focus on prayer and study and service and a big, intellectual God and a Bible full of Greek roots, I was forgetting that my God is a God who stoops down in love right now, even in the most personal of ways. I think for example of God's kindness in giving us the beautiful metaphor of a bird. The freedom of a bird is such a sharp contrast to the dark entrapment that Jack's body endured. When we think of Jack, we will be able to think of his soul soaring.

Each connection, each glimpse of the supernatural, is an astonishing display of tender, personal love, and that's what I want others to know, even if they don't experience them firsthand. Even when there are no signs, God is still close. But with signs, we are sometimes able to glimpse a little bit of the mystery of God in a way that amazes and encourages us right where we are.

Signs remind me that the God I believe in is active right now, pouring compassion out on my own little hurting life. And that Jack's soul is alive and well. I take them not as a shout, but as a caress, or a holy whisper: *"I'm here... Never will I leave you or forsake you... Didn't Jack say nothing is impossible with God?"*

thirty-four

I open the church bookstore one night hoping a major orchestra concert will bring in new customers. It's one of my first attempts to be out of the house in the evening after such a long time, and it feels okay. Only a handful of people wander in.

A couple in their late sixties or early seventies enters, and I ask how I can help them. They're holding hands. "Do you have any books on grief?"

"Sure." I lead them to the section in the back I've built up over the past two years, never guessing I'd be working through the titles for my own benefit, looking for a solution, a plan, a glimmer of hope.

"You sure have a big selection," the man says. "Have you read most of them?"

"Yes." I don't elaborate. Within five minutes these people will be out the door. They don't need my life story. Besides, I still haven't actually had to tell anyone what happened to Jack yet. In our small town most people already know, and it's not like I'm getting out and meeting new people every day. I dread saying the words just as I dread having to answer the question, "How many children do you have?" It will be six more months before my dental hygienist's persistent, "How's Jack?" and "I haven't seen Jack in a while" force me to finally say, with her hands in my mouth, "He died."

"We met in a grief group at our church," the man continues. "Her husband and my wife died a few months apart. Now we're getting married!" Ah, the hand holding. These two are newly in love. The woman looks from him to me, trying to get a pulse on whether his chatty behavior is annoying me. I wonder how hard it has been for her to embrace the promise of this new life while still honoring the life she had before.

I'm not annoyed. As long as this stays about them. But no, he plunges forward. "So have you had someone close to you die? I mean, if you've read all those books?" Fine. I'll say it. "My twelve-year-old son." I know if I say Jack's name, I'll burst into tears.

They look at each other again. I can see the woman considers cutting him off. Sparing me. But she doesn't. He looks at me, excitedly. "Your *son*? Oh, I'm so sorry. But then you must know now, don't you?"

"Know what?"

"How close they are! You know that, right?"

He doesn't wait for an answer. He gestures to his fiancée. "Her son heard her husband's voice on the phone. The phone! I mean, how does that work? And I saw my wife in my bedroom! *Saw* her! Isn't God good?"

A few months or even a few weeks ago, I would have written them off as crackpots. But now I know what they are saying is true. I know what they know, even though I certainly don't know how it all works. Our loved ones are closer than we think. The veil between "here" and "there" is very thin. The eternal life we talk about in our churches is real and it's going on right now.

All I can think of is, *Blessed are those who mourn, for they will be comforted.* This man wants to make sure I've been comforted, that I know the comfort is right under my nose and all around me through our loving God. His excitement at talking to someone else who, having lost so much, must surely understand makes me guess that his enthusiasm may not have been as well received in other circles.

And I get that. We try to figure out when to speak up and when to hold back.

But I'm also wary of holding back, because like this older gentleman, I want to spread the comfort around instead of keeping it to myself. I think that's part of Jack's mission in heaven, and I want to support him.

We are a secret society of believers tonight, here in the back corner of a church bookstore. There's no handshake for those of us who know, just a grief so profound that our eyes are open in a way they never have had to be before. With a tug of a hand and a smile, they are out the door.

IV

tomorrow
and tomorrow

thirty-five

I hate you!" I sneer at Tim when he climbs back into the car. I've never said these ugly words to him before.

"Of course you do! I've never done one damn thing right the whole time you've known me!" he yells back, the ugliest look I've ever seen on his face, his eyes a mixture of disgust and despair. Margaret stands outside the car, wailing and dry heaving in the filthy gas station parking lot. I spew angry words at Tim about his wanting to leave so late and about his herky-jerky driving. He says, "Maybe we should just forget the whole thing!"

"You need to go back out there and help her," I say. And he climbs out of the car.

We're trying to get to Richmond, two hours from our home, so Margaret can go to grief camp. It's exactly six months since Jack's accident, and despite God's love and Jack's signs and the support of our friends and family, we are in the weeds. The camp is for kids who have lost a parent or sibling, and we've heard amazing things about the caring way they reach kids and help them realize they aren't alone. All the counselors, or "big buddies," have experienced loss themselves, and there are professional therapists in each group who take the kids through healing exercises.

Turns out with a shocking death like Jack's, it takes many months before you can even begin to wrap your brain around what happened, let alone start to heal. The grief camp won't even consider kids who have experienced a loss fewer than four months before. So here we are at the six-month mark, pain pounding down on all of us, determined to get to Richmond, desperate to find a way to support our little girl.

I want to leave early in the morning and then hang around in Richmond, shopping and eating for a few hours before camp starts that evening. Tim is afraid that will give Margaret more opportunity to get anxious and refuse to go, so he wants to leave in the afternoon.

I'm pissed.

We leave in the afternoon and soon get into epic traffic on 95 South. Tim's pissed too, as if I have somehow caused this traffic jam as part of my diabolical plan to discredit him and blame him for all the problems in the world. He tries to get off the highway to take a shortcut. The stop-and-go lurching of traffic makes an already anxious Margaret feel like she's going to puke. Throwing up is her worst fear in the world. She says she would rather die than puke, and I believe her.

Her face becomes red and her body turns hot. She is starting to panic. We veer off into the gas station parking lot. It has taken us nearly three hours to get to Woodbridge, which is only twenty-three miles from our house. Car exhaust, trash, and the smell of greasy chicken greet us beside the road, cars whizzing by. Why they're going so fast now when all afternoon they've been at a standstill I could not tell you. Little Margaret, at barely four feet tall, weeps and wails and retches. Tim climbs out of the car, rubs her back, and tries to talk her down.

Because she usually turns to me when she is afraid, it is Tim's first opportunity to deal with one of Margaret's full-blown, fear-induced, "I'm going to be sick" episodes, when she'll stand holding my hand, not moving any part of her flushed red body, afraid that the slightest movement will cause her to vomit. She has me pray for her and read psalms aloud as she tries not to shake. Now I sit in the car, my head on the steering wheel, as Tim gently talks Margaret through some deep breathing.

The family at the roadside in Woodbridge is unrecognizable to me. We are turning on one another like caged animals. I wonder whether we should push ahead with camp. Tim is ready to throw in the towel, but I feel strongly that the camp will be good for Margaret. But am I forcing it just so I can look like I'm doing something for her? So I can have an answer when people ask me if we are getting her help? What the hell do I know about parenting at this point?

Who am I kidding that I can make good decisions for our family? Look where we've ended up!

I lift my head and say aloud the strange words that are buzzing around in my head, "Satan, you cannot have this family! Satan, you cannot have this family!" It sounds odd to say it out loud, and the family I'm talking about just seems like a tattered, broken remnant of family anyway, but I say the words and sink back into my seat.

Tim and Margaret get back in the car, and I know I need to make the decision, since I've moved over to the driver's seat. North means home; south means camp. As smoothly as possible, I head south. Margaret's mood has shifted completely, as has Tim's. By the time we get to the secluded camp, a two-hour drive has taken more than six hours. Camp is well underway, and it would be easy to back out now. Margaret says calmly, knowing we are more apt to reason with her if she's reasonable with us, "Please don't make me go."

It is after 7 p.m. I know she has not eaten since 11 a.m., had even one sip of water, or gone to the bathroom. My heart is breaking as I lead her to her counselor, give her a quick kiss on the head, turn, and walk away.

Tim and I spend the weekend worrying about Margaret at camp. Is she sleeping? Does she feel betrayed? We're staying at a hotel just twenty minutes away in case she needs us. In the past a childless trip to a hotel would have been a minivacation. This time, we cry silently and play word games on our phones, go out to dinner, and try to think of nonworried things to say to each other. Later, we will make ourselves fool around. The ugliness from the car ride is gone; now we just need to make it to pickup time. We also have the impossible task of trying to dodge the more than one hundred boisterous thirteen-year-old boys and their families who are staying in the hotel for a weekend soccer tournament. Seriously.

When we pick Margaret up, she's beaming. She's not going to be one of those kids who hugs her counselor, crying, saying she doesn't want to leave this little cocoon of love. No, she's ready to leave, but despite the trauma of getting here, hiding her light from others would have been impossible. Even shaken and stunned, Margaret's spunk and humor and spirit can't be extinguished. She has participated willingly in her group and given other kids support as they shared their own losses.

I'll furtively glimpse at a list she made at camp, of how she feels without Jack, and see the words: *shocked, bewildered, misunderstood,* and *lonely,* and I'll be amazed to see so much of my own grief experience summed up by a ten-year-old.

The campers' nametags are covered with metal pins that participants give out over the weekend when you do something particularly brave or contribute something valuable to the group as a whole. "I forgive you for making me come here," Margaret says, handing me her sleeping bag. As she walks to open the car door, I see her nametag is weighed down by row after row of pins.

"Man, looks like you got the most pins in the whole camp," I whisper to her.

"I know," she whispers back, looking pretty satisfied.

thirty-six

"D on't say it, Mom," Margaret says, annoyed, as I start the car after yet another soccer game. A father in a Jeep does doughnuts in the gravel parking lot, a girl of five or six standing on top of the headrest, hanging out the roof up to her waist. Margaret knows what I want to say—that it's asinine that absolutely nothing is going to happen to this little girl, despite her father's reckless behavior, but that our son is dead.

She knows, because everywhere we go these days, I seem to encounter this kind of scene. A mother dangling a lit cigarette in her baby's face, little hands grasping at the burning ember. A little girl sitting on the curb chatting up day laborers who are there to spread her neighbor's mulch. A child lying down in the middle of the street, barely visible as I round the corner in my car. Boys jumping up and down on the roof of a rotting storage shed outside my family room window. A small child in the toy aisle of Target, no parents in sight.

Every scene is one of potential peril. I hold my breath in fear, but each time the moment passes and all is well. Do I spend my life crusading for these little ones, knowing what I now know, that anything could happen? Do I approach parents as a harbinger of doom, checking their children's car-seat straps, knocking baby bottles full of Coke out of their hands, and sending little wanderers back to their mothers? I don't know.

I was raised as a free-range kid, and I survived. These kids will survive too. Unless they don't. And I surely can't predict it. It doesn't seem fair that some children come out of dangerous situations unscathed, while others don't. I guess I'm still wrestling with my erroneous belief that if I tried hard and worried enough, my kids would be safe from harm and we could have had the kind of future I dreamed about after my mom died. I was stable and reliable. I was protective and tuned in. My kids were responsible. And yet. And yet.

I know this is a fruitless, worthless argument—that my kids somehow deserve to be alive because of my good intentions as a mother. Does a loving mom who lives on a dangerous block have the luxury of the false assumptions of safety that I had, when regardless of what she does, her child could still be hit by an errant bullet at any time? What about a child growing up in poverty in Afghanistan or in Somalia? His mother's desires are no less important than mine!

What about when the danger comes from within, from cancer or a genetic illness? Did Jack have more of a right to live because he was 100 percent healthy at the time of the accident? And what about the babies buckled snugly into car-safety seats who still die? Their mothers could do nothing more to protect them.

The truth is, it's not fair. None of it. It's not fair that many children survive and thrive despite risky childhoods, but I'm thankful that they do. Children also usually survive the less obvious momentary lapses in judgment we all make, when we let go of a hand for an instant, when we turn our heads away for a second, when we get distracted by life. If I'm truly honest with myself, I can think of other times when I could have lost one or both of my children over the years, long before I lost Jack.

Children die in flooded creeks, hospital beds, refugee camps, and the family minivan. It happens. I fear I may have another lesson in letting go. I don't want to let go of our past. I don't want to let go of the family I dreamed of and worked for and prayed for. And I don't want to let go of this idea of fairness that somehow lingers from my childhood, even though it now feels stupid. Because it says that I can do something. That my love and hard work and what I pour into my children will amount to what I think it should. But when I get caught up trying to make life fair, it threatens to mire me in anger and bitterness.

Where does faith fit in? Can I somehow have faith that God sees the bigger picture? That justice is His job, not mine? That He will make all things beautiful in His time? That I was not put here to play God, to decide who is safe enough and who is reckless, who lives and who dies?

Even at ten years old, Margaret understands the futility of the road I'm going down as I try to argue with the way things are.

"Don't say it, Mom…," she says, because identifying others' shortcomings and trying to justify my parenting won't bring back Jack.

And though my mothering did not turn out the way I wanted, with both my kids growing up safely, it did matter. It was not wasted or stupid. The balance of freedom and security, humor and structure, that was our family culture, modeled after what I learned from my own mom, made us who we were, and I have to believe there was good in that. Even if that meant playing in the rain.

thirty-seven

I n late spring the cemetery association sends us a letter pointing out that we have yet to erect a gravestone. If we do not have one by the one-year mark, the cemetery will place a plain flat marker there for us, for a fee.

Margaret, too, has noted that we haven't yet taken care of this detail. I'm sure to her it seems as if we just can't get our acts together to mark where Jack's ashes are buried and replace the cheap plastic marker with something substantial. And getting our acts together *has* been difficult. I still have less energy and gumption than before. Tim is plodding along doing what he needs to do and has continued to pick up my slack—paying the bills I used to pay, making runs to the store, and helping Margaret with her math.

But the something "extra" of trying to figure out how to capture who Jack was on a slab of granite seems like too much for either of us. I've been telling people we are following the Jewish tradition of waiting one year, not because we are Jewish, but because I haven't been able to face it yet.

Of course I think deep down I am just morally opposed to any parent having to commemorate the spot where her child is buried, because I don't think moms should have to bury their children. Ever. So Jack's blank grave is, in a way, my silent protest.

Not that mothers haven't been doing this since the beginning of time, placing rocks or crude wooden crosses on top of tiny mounds of dirt all around the world—if they were fortunate enough to know their children's resting places. In fact, many mothers have not had the opportunity that I have.

They've had to leave their children behind on a wagon trail, in a concentration camp, in a jungle or a desert, in any number of unthinkable circumstances, with no chance to mark or revisit the spot. I am fortunate that the cemetery is in my town and that the small wooden box of ashes, along with three tiny Lego pieces, is buried right next to my mom.

As a college student, I would drive her old minivan to the cemetery in the dying light, startling the deer with my headlights, and walk over to her grave. Sometimes I would cry. Other times I would just pat the stone, look around a little, get back in the car, and drive away.

Even at dusk, I could see that some graves were unmarked, except for the cheap plastic nameplates from the funeral homes. Many were several years old, covered with dirt and grass clippings. This must have been before the strict one-year rule was adopted. My college-age self felt sorry for the people buried there. They seemed so neglected. I figured their families were too poor to buy a stone or had forgotten about their loved ones entirely.

Now I realize that cemeteries are different for different people. My grandparents take solace in visiting my uncle, their beloved son, at the cemetery where he is buried. They go nearly every day. Tim, Margaret, and I have still only been a few times since we buried Jack.

Tim and I are rule followers, and I'm sure we will obey the one-year requirement. Jack's grave will eventually have some sort of stone. I do want to have a place people can go to pay their respects to Jack, where it can be whatever it needs to be for them.

I think I'm going to see if a stone bench will fit there, instead of a headstone, so I can continue my protest in a small way yet provide a place for someone to sit, pray, laugh, or cry.

The process seems paralyzing and leaves me with questions.

How do you capture the sparkle in an eye? a contagious laugh? wit? wisdom? a pat on a sister's back? How do you show a love of logic and math coupled with words, words, and more words? an introvert? a leader? the world's softest cheek? Can we truly convey the essence of someone who touched so many lives in twelve years, but should have had about seventy-one more to do it in?

Of course not. It's hard to fathom how we will make these choices. So we wait.

I guess sometimes those little plastic markers really do say a lot. Just not what I thought they did.

thirty-eight

D iana and our childhood friend Brenda are back in town visiting family. We head out to one of our old high school haunts. Sitting in a sticky diner booth, we talk about Jack, still disbelieving that he's gone. And as we rehash what happened, we feel the echo of an earlier loss.

I'll never forget having to call and tell them that my mother was dead. We were just eighteen, too young to be dealing with matters of life and death. Brenda and Diana recognized the enormity of the loss, and all these years they've been sensitive to me as I've faced milestone after milestone without my mother. They never forgot what I was missing.

Now I realize I have yet another gulf separating my friends and me. Not only can they still enjoy the support of their moms right now, but they will be able to see their children reach adulthood. Their children will grow and flourish. Jack will be forever twelve. And spunky, spirited Margaret will have a life tinged with loss.

Around this same time I hear the terms *collateral damage* and *secondary losses* in some of the grief books I read and realize they give a name to the wider gulf between my friends and me as well as the many other losses we discover after losing Jack.

It seems if you lose a child—or suffer some other major disaster—you and your family should get a free pass on absolutely everything else. Money issues should disappear. Surviving children should flourish. Your marriage should grow stronger. You'll be closer to your friends than ever.

But instead, collateral losses pile up. Of course there's the loss of being a mom of a boy and the stab of pain when other moms joke about smelly socks, annoying video games, and not being able to keep enough food in the house.

We're having a hard time finishing a gallon of milk in a week, and much of our food goes bad before we have a chance to eat it. I haven't yet gotten the hang of shopping for three, and the grocery store remains the place most likely to bring me to tears.

Without my boy, I'll never have a reason to go to the barbershop again. Would I ever just walk in to say hi to the barbers I've known since Jack was two? At least Tim can still go in there to get a haircut. What is it like for him? Boys of any age send me spiraling into pain because when I see them, I miss toddler Jack, little-boy Jack, twelve-year-old Jack, and the teenager he was so close to becoming.

There's the loss of a middle schooler. I've been at this parenting gig just as long as my friends have, yet they've moved forward to algebra and Spanish and I'm held back in elementary school with Margaret. It's impossible not to hear about the field trips and adventures Jack's classmates are going on, and each time I do, I want to die. Not to kill myself, just to have a black hole open up on the road one day and swallow my car and me whole so I don't have to feel this pain.

When it comes time to consider where Margaret should go to middle school, I am angry that I don't have Jack's experience to draw upon. Instead, I will have to call friends and ask their advice or schedule a meeting with the principals. If Jack were at our kitchen table, I'd already know the scoop.

I feel a loss of credibility as a mother. Can I still weigh in on parenthood, as a friend and a "mommy blogger," when I've lost my child? I feel diminished. A sense of shame and despair hangs over me. I wonder if people want to avoid me because I represent their deepest, unspoken fears. I'm pretty sure I would.

Then there's the loss of baseball, Boy Scouts, church youth groups, and the many relationships that were based around Jack. It's so complicated. Jack's friends' parents are our friends. Do we talk about their kids, or will that make them feel guilty for what they have and we don't? Do I resent their kids for being alive? I think I do, and it doesn't feel good. I don't want all the other adolescent boys dead; I just want mine to be alive. What a freaking mess.

Tim and I try to go to a baseball game to support Jack's old team and to watch his friend Davis play, but our pain is so raw we do nothing but cry. We don't take Margaret along because we're trying to shield her from times we know all eyes will be on us. She already feels weird enough as the girl with the dead brother. "When everyone looks at us, I feel like an alien," she says.

And we realize Margaret not only lost her best friend and brother, with their private jokes and secret conversations, but she loses the laid-back comings and goings of boys in our house and her life. There is no longer a stinky shoe pile by the kitchen door, no stream of boys coming in and out during the day. No easy joking with the opposite sex.

How meaningful it was to me when I was growing up to get to know my brother's friends this way. Having an older brother made me feel protected, demystified boys to me, and vastly improved my social life.

"Jack would have been my hot older brother," Margaret says one day, missing Jack, her protector and encourager, but also something else he could have brought to the table during her teen years.

I wonder, is Margaret still a sister if her brother is gone?

From childhood we consider our lives in relation to others: mother, daughter, spouse, sister, friend. When those relationships break or disappear, where does that leave us? How do we integrate the loss into our identities, holding on to what the relationship means, while finding a way to move forward?

Someone points out to me that there is no label or title for a person who has lost a child. *Widow, widower,* or *orphan* won't do. Is this lack because child loss is so repugnant, so out of the natural order of things, it can scarcely be named? Can we not dig and find a Latin or Greek root that could lead us to a term for ourselves?

I'm not sure if labels help anyway, as we struggle to figure out our identities in light of loss.

I remember thinking about this when my mother died, because even though Margaret Whiston was gone, I was not ready to stop being her daughter. I wonder if this is why I ended up staying in my hometown as an adult, and even kept my maiden name, for those times over the years, infrequent but cherished, when people made the connection and said, "Oh! I loved your mother!" and offered up a memory at the supermarket register or across a church pew.

In those moments I was still Margaret Whiston's daughter, and it felt good to be known.

These days, I may be Anna the writer, the mother, the sister, the wife, the friend, but I still need to be known as "Jack's mom" too. It's one collateral loss that I'm just not willing to accept.

During the first year after Jack's death, some losses show themselves immediately; others unfold over days and weeks. Occasionally, I let myself feel the composite impact of all these losses, but then I must pull back again, because it is too much. Instead, I ask for the strength to get through this one moment and hang on until the next time impossible hope shows up.

One day I am at a Mexican restaurant in a neighboring town with Margaret, Tim, my dad, my stepmother, and others. It's a big dinner. I even order beer instead of my usual water, assuming my dad will pick up the bill. At the end of our meal, the server comes over and says our meal has already been paid for.

A stranger who most likely read my blog found a way to honor our past and our present that went far beyond just paying for our dinner. Her message for our server was, "Tell them it's for Jack's mom."

thirty-nine

We have two showers in our house. The one in our tiny master bathroom is our favorite. All four of us used it, ever since the kids graduated from baths. Even Shadow gets shampooed in there.

The shower has the perfect water pressure—hard, but not "I just lost a nipple down the drain" hard. Superhot—just on this side of scalding. Liz even invokes her sisterly privilege to use it when she visits.

Sometimes, when we were in a hurry, I'd see if the kids would use the other perfectly serviceable shower, and occasionally Margaret would oblige, but Jack refused. The kids' shower was newer, their bathroom brighter and more spacious, but the water pressure and showering experience just could not compare.

Not long ago I noticed a leak from the good shower down into the powder room below. Now we are left with a ripped-up ceiling and a shower that needs fixing. We don't have the the energy to deal with it.

So the three of us must traipse up to the kids' shower. While at first I can't imagine using the lesser shower instead of the one just a few steps from my bed, I know I must. After several weeks the new morning routine becomes just another part of my day.

It makes me think of Jack. Well, doesn't *everything*?

Our new life is a poor substitution for the life we wanted for our family. We trudge along, in a world that seems warped, trying to adapt and make the most of what lies before us. That doesn't mean we like it. It doesn't mean we don't consider what came before to be far, far superior.

But we do it, out of necessity, and bit by bit we get used to it. Now that the days since the accident have turned into months and are approaching a year, I've got to say it would seem a little strange to have Jack suddenly show up. To tell us how the middle school dance went. To talk Margaret into playing outside again.

Because we have started to adapt to his absence. I suppose you can get used to almost anything.

forty

Grievers I've come across function within society, and most days it appears pretty seamless. We volunteer at church. We go to school plays. We shop. We cheer from the sidelines. We try to blend in. We smile. We look normal. We need people to feel okay being open and natural around us, so as not to drive us even further apart from the world. We are not from another planet, but it feels that way, so far removed is our experience from those around us.

There is a constant undercurrent of loss, a schism in our brains, which we gradually learn to adapt to, but is ever present. It's as if our brains are operating on two separate tracks. One is the here and now. The second is the parallel track of what could or should have been yet will not be. Most days I can keep the second track hidden. Other times, I haven't got a prayer.

Like when Tim and I sit in plastic cafeteria chairs watching Margaret play Lucy in a fifth-grade production of *The Lion, the Witch, and the Wardrobe*. Two years ago, the last time the school put on this play, Jack played the part of Edmund, Lucy's older brother. We'd passed the script around the kitchen table, helping him practice. I always read the witch's lines, and Margaret read Lucy's, hoping she would land that part when she reached fifth grade.

And she does. She's the perfect Lucy and utterly believable as she annoys her older brother and then searches for him desperately when he disappears. We are enormously proud of her talents, but watching it quickly knocks me onto that second track of *should*.

Jack *should* be here watching Margaret. They *should* have been able to practice together and talk about the ways the play is different this year. He *should* be sitting in the back of the cafeteria with his middle school classmates, their growing bodies taking up too much space in these dinky chairs, under the watchful eyes of their teachers.

In the play, when Lucy scours Narnia, calling out for Edmund, the symbolism is not lost on us. And when the lion, Aslan, lays down his life so that Edmund may live, we are of course thinking: Edmund/Lucy, Jack/Margaret.

I'm already crying, but I cry even harder when I see the playbill:

"Dedicated to the memory of Jack Harris Donaldson, with Aslan."

Of course, we knew that this play was going to be difficult. But it's just one example of how people in grief experience life on two tracks. Most days we are able to operate on the level of the here and now, but sometimes the other part comes to the forefront.

I could never have imagined being in this club. Just the summer before the accident, I heard of a child in our town falling off a horse and dying. It seemed so bizarre. So tragic. Trying to distance myself from the terrifying thought that I, too, could have a child die, I quickly justified in my head, *Well, at least Jack and Margaret don't ride horses.* Less than a year later, I'll be sitting in that boy's kitchen, talking to his mom, because of our most unwelcome bond.

But first I resist. I do not want to believe that Jack is dead. I do not want to talk to other parents who have lost a child. And I certainly do not want to be one of them! I find this out when Tim and I go to a meeting for bereaved parents just a few weeks after the accident. We come out depressed and depleted, determined never to go back.

We are still in shock but also in a state of being tenderly held up by the Spirit of God. We seek hope and meaning in Jack's death, and we are so earnest in our naive desire to "be okay!" and "get better!" quickly for Jack's sake and ours that the meeting feels like a setback. To see parents who are still suffering greatly, many years after their children died, gives us a window into a despair we don't want to see. Surely we will feel better than they did at five years out!

Now I understand that the monthly meeting is their safe place. Their pain and desire to tell their stories didn't mean they weren't functioning in society, holding jobs, and taking care of their families. It just meant that during the day in and day out of living with and adapting to the two-track existence of life and loss, those meetings were one place to openly talk about the track that is less visible but very present.

I've reached the point where I realize I do need spaces to do the hard work of grieving. I need to turn over ideas in my head, hold them up to the light, and examine them as I cry out in longing for the boy who should be with me in body, not just in spirit. My blog is one space to do this, and eventually, so is talking to other grieving mothers, aliens like me.

Sitting around an outdoor table, eating taco salad, laughing, and drinking margaritas from one of those tabletop margarita machines, we look like normal women. Five suburban moms together on a Virginia evening. The only reason we know one another is because our sons are dead. Jack died in a creek. Owen fell off a horse. Jacob had an epileptic seizure. Steve and Richie had cancer. We're at Linda's house, on a patio overlooking her expansive, rolling yard. The yard where a helicopter landed to airlift her son to the hospital. We found one another through the grapevine, through friends of friends, "I know a woman..."

This group is where we talk about our sons. It's where we feel less strange because we are all in the same situation. Jane shares that she's less tolerant of other people's crap these days. "I thought I'd be more loving after losing Steve, but, really, I get more easily fed up." We nod in agreement. It's hard to listen to people's seemingly petty concerns when we've buried our children. Sheryl admits that while she feels bad for people who lost kids younger than her son, who was twelve, she's envious of those who had their children even a year or two longer. Kate, whose son died at nineteen, takes no offense. "I'd feel the same way. It's hard to imagine if I'd lost Richie when he was twelve." We nod, all wishing we'd had more time. A few more years, hours, or even minutes.

We repeat ourselves, telling the minute details of our sons' deaths. It's no longer okay to do this in other circles, but we can do it here. Revisiting those moments. Trying to make sense of them, squinting as if the synapses in our brains are working overtime. As the months go on, this need lessens considerably, but we know that we can and will retell the stories here. Not because the others need to hear one more time that I let the kids play in the rain that night, that I was this close to saving my son, but because I may need to say it out loud again.

I'm not sure how sharing the broken, hurting pieces of our lives helps us, but it does. Rather than wallowing in despair, this group of scrappy women cheers each other on, determined to find a way to live the lives we have now. And in sharing our loss, we somehow gain. That is the mystery of a community of grievers.

forty-one

Margaret and I find a yellow folder with page after page of Jack's handwriting from when he was nine or ten years old. The pages are a "Dream Chart" he created, then filled out for seventy days. The first page has a key with two components—a color and a number—with which he rated his dreams each morning.

Green = Funny
Blue = Happy
Red = Scary
Purple = Weird or Other

After the color, came an overall score:

1 = Terrible
2 = Bad
3 = OK (not bad, medium)
4 = Good
5 = Great :)

The next seven pages, labeled "Jack 1" through "Jack 7," each list ten dreams and their ratings. Examples include:

Scaffolding: "Red, 1" or Scary, Terrible
Exhibit of Fun: "Blue, 5" or Happy, Great
Bounding, Swirling, and Slipping: "Green, 5" or Funny, Great
Bee Mom: "Red, 1" or Scary, Terrible
Public School: "Red, 4" or Scary, Good

Jack's Dream Chart represents what I love about him. It shows persever-ance, as I can't think of very many things I've voluntarily kept up with for seventy straight days. It is quirky and creative. And the way Jack maintained this list each day, while his dreams were still fresh, reminds me of the way he operated at home: quietly, methodically, always thinking.

Mostly, it makes me consider how sometimes the worst moments can be tied to the best, like "Red, 4" or "Scary, Good." Jack's rating system gives me permission to feel two things at once and view life less simplistically than be-fore. This seems to allow for the complexities of grief.

Like how going to the grocery store nearly kills me, but that's where I hap-pen to see Mrs. Davidson and she gives me a bit of hope that this will somehow get easier. How being in our house brings comfort because it is Jack's home, but it hurts so much that I can't seem to thrive here anymore. How Jack's death has brought many people closer to God and to their children, but has left us lonely and bereft. How I can feel disappointed at God in the same moment that I marvel at His care for me.

Losing Jack brought us more pain yet at the same time more comfort than my small mind could have imagined. Death has broken some relationships but has brought us richer ones as well.

And just as my son has never spent such a long time away from me, out of reach of my hugs, in some ways he may be even closer to me than he ever could be before. Maybe I just needed a more complex rating system.

forty-two

We begin visiting a different church. We don't feel Jack's absence as keenly here, even though it meets in a local elementary school in the same room where he attended Cub Scout pack meetings for five years.

We go at first to support the young pastor who showed up for us the night of Jack's death, but then we keep coming. I have yet to tell him about a conversation I had with my pastor Linda three hours before the accident.

"Did you know there's a new church coming to Vienna this fall?" I asked. She didn't. I continued, "Well, I was reading their website during lunch, and I have a feeling we'll be connected to them somehow."

Strange. I guess I thought we could lend the church space in our building or maybe I would help them order materials for their Sunday school classes. Looking around the elementary school cafeteria now, months later, I know I got it wrong. I see two friends who recommitted their lives to God after Jack's accident and started bringing their families here. I see the family we went to the beach with summer after summer when the kids were small, who understand what a precious person we lost in losing Jack. I see his math teacher, who got to teach him for only the first two days of seventh grade, but who is helping shepherd his classmates through their grief.

I see men who put on raincoats and traipsed through the mud, thinking surely they would find Jack injured but alive. And there are the couples who formed small groups in our neighborhood initially to talk about God and the death of a young boy, but who continue to meet and support one another week after week as more deaths and cancer diagnoses rock our small community. We are connected to this new church, just not in the way I had expected.

I don't know if this is where we belong, but I'm open to it, even though I have worshiped in the same church my entire life. I'm not worried. What would have once seemed like a sea change feels more like a blip in comparison to losing Jack.

And whether I'm here or across town, I need church. I am not one who regularly sees God at the ocean, in the mountains, or in a sunrise, although since Jack died, I am increasingly finding Him there. God and I tend to meet in community, and even though I dread the exposed and vulnerable feeling I get walking into His house now, I can't stay away.

It has nothing to do with obligation or religion. I need to show up, sit on the hard plastic chair, and say, "Here I am, Lord." For me. I sing when I can, but I don't push it if I don't feel up to it. Margaret sometimes moves up to the front rows where the tweens sit, and I feel more freedom to cry than I do from our exposed perch in the balcony of our home church where my emotions continue to embarrass her.

The pastor, Johnny, jokes with Tim that he knows when we'll visit because when we do, they always seem to have Jack and Margaret's favorite hymn, "In Christ Alone," on the schedule. They'll start the music, he'll scan the congregation, and bingo, there we are, wiping dripping eyes and noses with the back of our sleeves, because even though crying is inevitable, I don't always remember tissues.

It feels a bit weird to be at a different church, even just part-time, but if we're learning anything, it's that life is weird. I take communion, but I don't serve it anymore. I am not here as a leader or a giver. I don't go out of my way to meet new people and make them feel welcome and comfortable, as would be my instinct. Instead, I am here to partake and absorb and let God's words fall down on my head. I soak up the truth of who He is. I tell Him I am open to receive grace and comfort. I remind Him I trust Him, even though His ways are not mine and I am still sad and hurt.

I don't know if I'll speak at women's retreats again or lead Bible studies. I don't know how long I'll work in a church. The look of my faith may be changing in light of Jack's death, as I step back from what I saw as *my* work and *my* effort of growing closer to God and being a good Christian, but God hasn't changed. It seems like this is a season for me to rest in love and just keep showing up.

V

nothing
is impossible

forty-three

Courtney and I are out to lunch. It has been months since we've seen each other. Her baby sits between us, opening her mouth for small bites of guacamole. Courtney tells me she senses a quieter, calmer Jack these days. I don't like the sound of that. Where is the exuberance, the awe, the wonder? Has his early fear come true and he is now bored with heaven?

When I call Liz later that day, she responds immediately with, "Sounds like Home Jack to me." Home Jack? It does. We could never figure out why Jack was so quiet, serious, and focused at home, yet so playful at school, to the annoyance of more than one teacher. Tim and I would get frustrated, because we knew he could be diligent, so why would he choose to stir up his classmates and make them laugh at all the worst moments? Why did he get up once during math class and start eating his lunch? Who does that?

But then I think of Jack's classmates, who were his closest friends, and I wonder if any of this could have served a purpose. Even a small one. So that when these young kids experienced the first big loss of their lives, they could look back at Jack Donaldson and remember him with laughter, the kind of laughter that makes your stomach hurt and tears stream down your face.

Yes, they would also have cared about a quiet, obedient kid in the corner, but would they have had the stories to tell? Would they have been able to say with confidence that they really knew him and he was a big part of their lives? This handful of kids had been together since they were six years old, so I'm sure they remember the other parts of Jack too: artistic, smart, tearful, humble, easily frustrated, kind. But I think it's the laughter they'll remember most.

Maybe Liz is right, and Jack is more settled now in his new home.

"I sense that he's being quiet and he's listening," Courtney says.

"For what?"

"Do you ever talk to Jack?"

"No, not really." I'd never talked to my mother after she'd died either. I mean, what would I say?

She continues, "Well, it seems like he's listening."

I'm just starting to grasp the words I hear at funerals: "Death ends a life not a relationship. So-and-So is more alive today than he ever has been." How many times have I heard this? Twenty? Fifty? I realize I've never lived like I believed any of it. *More alive?* If I can believe it now, maybe that changes everything.

I begin to talk to Jack. When I drive around and see the blue ribbons that still flutter on mailboxes and trees, I start to say, "I love you, Jack. I love you, honey," sometimes out loud, sometimes in my head. It feels good to speak into the silence. I know he always knew I loved him, was crazy about him, really, but it feels good to say the words in present tense. Because my love is not in the past. The day after the accident, I gasped to no one in particular, "But I loved him so much!" incredulous that someone so beloved could go away. Now, I realize I *love* him so much. That will not change.

I start to talk to him when I mow the grass. I don't say a lot, mainly just, "I'm sorry, buddy" and "I love you." We used to hire people to mow our grass. I loved coming home to a freshly mowed lawn, with the leaves and helicopter seeds blown off our driveway by an efficient team of workers.

Then we bought a new lawn mower and canceled the lawn guys, because at twelve, Jack was old enough to take over the job. His weight was still hovering in the sixties the last summer of his life, finally hitting seventy pounds the week he died. He took to the job quickly and enjoyed earning extra money to save up for Legos.

After the accident Tim and I eventually pick the mowing back up again.

"Do you remember it being this hard?" I ask Tim.

"No. The roots and the hills! Our yard is so steep. How did he do it?" Tim wonders, shaking his head.

We are silent. We both feel remorse. Jack hadn't complained, so we didn't know what a challenge our yard must have been for him at his small size. I remember his asking one day if he could get the mowing over with while I was at work. "No, it's too dangerous. Stay inside and wait 'til I get home." I pictured his losing a thumb to the blade like my friend Patrick had or running over his foot.

Now Tim and I take turns. I push the mower up over high, high roots, cursing as I use all my strength. I roll past the garden bed, along a steep slope, and feel the tension as the mower tilts and threatens to tip me over, down the hill. I let out a moan of exertion as I push through the tall grass. "I miss you," I grunt, my voice drowned out by the mower.

I wonder what it was like for him, at half my size, to do this job. "I'm sorry, buddy," I say as I crisscross the yard. "I didn't know." Jack's and my relationship was based on huge love and respect, and I have very few regrets. It's as if we knew each other from the beginning of time and trusted each other explicitly.

I'd always told Jack he was the strongest person I knew, but I meant his inner, moral strength. Now I think about how he must have been physically stronger than I realized. He never got the chance to spend his mowing money, but he seemed to enjoy earning it.

Weird thoughts go through my head as I mow, such as how I'm glad I didn't let him mow that day when I wasn't home because "something bad" could have happened to him. And then I realize how stupid it is to still feel that relief now, when something really bad did happen just a few weeks later. Much more than losing a toe.

And I realize as I mow and talk to Jack, that when I say, "I'm sorry, buddy" and "I didn't know," that I'm probably not talking just about mowing anymore.

forty-four

The one-year "crapiversary" of Jack's accident approaches, and a feeling of doom settles down on us as we go through the motions of summer. Haven't we had many good days? Haven't we started to get better? The heaviness feels like the thick, warm air the day of the accident, but of course we didn't know then what the air portended. Now we do. We know more pain and heartbreak than we would have thought possible one year ago, when I naively found myself wanting to be less busy, to lose ten pounds, and have less laundry to do. I got all those things and a painful introduction to a life that I could not have imagined.

I ask my grief-group friends about the one-year mark. Did they feel as weepy and miserable as I do, the mantle of sadness pressing them lower, much lower than the prior few months of hope and healing? The discouraging consensus is that it often gets worse, temporarily, in the second year. Not worse as in it will never get better, but the second year can bring up hard, intense feelings that we may have thought we'd already worked through during the first year, having made it through Thanksgiving, Christmas, Mother's Day, and even a birthday. Grief isn't linear as I had imagined. I hear somewhere that it is more of a spiral, where we have to come to the same places, again and again, but each time we've risen a little farther out of the pit.

I am not going to resign myself to the second year being worse, but I'm not going to expect to feel healed just because we make it to the one-year mark either.

My biggest fear for the second year is leaving Jack further behind. I won't be able to say, "Exactly one year ago today, we were at the beach. One year ago was Jack's last baseball scrimmage. One year ago was the school play. This time last year we were at Walmart shopping for school supplies..." Dust will settle

on our family stories. Jack's face will stay young in his pictures. Soon Margaret
will age past him.

So I take my friends' experiences, not as a prescription for how my own
reaction to the crapiversary will be, but as permission to let it be what it will be.
To not expect that making it through a year will wrap anything up with a bow.

Tim and I are weepier than we've been. We struggle to make a decision
about the cemetery bench. When we get to the store, about twenty miles from
our home, they've forgotten our appointment and lost all the information about
Jack and his death that I've tearfully given over the phone. They put us with a
salesperson who is just "filling in" and knows nothing of our story. Tim and I
walk among the sample gravestones beside a traffic-clogged road. We settle on
something quickly and are assured that it will be delivered by the one-year mark.

And just like the other significant dates of the past year, I find the anticipation leading up to it, the dread that has rendered my entire August miserable,
is worse than the day itself. My sister and her kids come for a low-key visit. We
go to the cemetery to see the bench, and it's much easier to go with them than
just the three of us.

Liz gasps when she sees her own words carved into the stone, the list of life
lessons she learned from Jack: "Be Kind. Pay Attention. Think. Never Give
Up. Play. Share Others' Joy." There's a photo of him, taken just the day before
the accident, with the words, "Our Rare Bird" carved next to it. His head looks
a little crooked, leaning at an odd angle, and I realize it's because in the original
picture he's leaning toward Margaret, resting his head on hers. The picture is
now incomplete, and that seems pretty accurate. On the back of the bench is
Jack's Bible verse: "For nothing is impossible with God." What does it mean to
us today?

After the cemetery we head to Taco Bell and sit in our usual booth. The
mood is light and the three kids laugh and reminisce. Our stairstep children—
Isaac, Caroline, and Margaret—are finding a way to interact without the second step: Jack.

People have tied new blue ribbons all around town for today, boys put blue-ribbon decals on their football helmets, and some of Jack's friends pin ribbons on their baseball uniforms for the first game of the season. Each ribbon feels like love. It's a ridiculously gorgeous day, with the start of fall sports and the crisp feel of promise in the air.

Until the tornado warning. The sky grows dark, and we head to the basement to play board games and wait it out. I'm amazed at how quickly word gets out about this dangerous weather today, versus just one year ago when we were all caught completely off guard. The warning passes as quickly as it came, and we spend the rest of the early evening watching a movie. I'm in my pajamas before sunset.

After the sun goes down, my sister leads us out into our long driveway, even though I'm in my pj's. Up and down each side shine glowing luminaria, white paper sacks lit from within with a candle. Each sack has a message about Jack on it from a friend, teacher, neighbor, or coach. We walk up and down and read. That Jack matters. That he is not forgotten. It is breathtaking and beautiful.

Two doors down, our friends wait for us in an open garage, the same garage where Jenn sat as our kids played in the cul-de-sac that rainy day. Tonight there's a spread of food on card tables, and children run around. This is where they've come to pray for us and surprise us with the luminaria.

We thank them for their love, for the ways they have consciously chosen not to forget, for the way they've allowed themselves to be changed by Jack. They let themselves get muddy and wet that first night and in the entire year since. First by the rain, and then by tears and the messiness of grief, both ours and their own. These relationships and the friends all over the world who have supported us are in some ways the collateral gains of our losing Jack.

They show us the startling pictures on their phones they've taken earlier. As they had gathered at the same time of the accident one year before, the tornado warning passed. They ate dinner together and filled the paper sacks with sand, reading the loving messages on each one, before setting them out in our driveway. And at sunset, above the creek blazed an intense sky of pinks and purples and blues. In the other direction, right over our house at the top of the hill, while we sat inside, hung a brilliant double rainbow. It was 8 p.m., one year to the moment when Jack's body was found.

When Jack was in sixth grade, we pulled into the driveway and he said, "I think I might want to be a missionary, but I may be too shy."

Margaret replied, "I don't *ever* want to be a missionary. They have terrible toilets!"

Having been on a lot of mission trips, I knew she was right—the toilets weren't all that great. I told Jack that there are lots of ways of being a missionary even if you're shy.

I wonder, given the way he is still touching people's lives, even one year after his death, if Jack has become a missionary without ever having to say a word.

forty-five

Margaret has had a really bad day. Her energy level, like mine, is still low. She needs to start working on a project for school. Forty dollars worth of supplies from the craft store later, and she is ready to begin. She molds mountains out of clay on the kitchen counter. I walk by and say, "Maybe you could make a few of the mountains a little taller so they'll look bigger than the trees."

Wailing, weeping, blaming. I've tainted her project that she worked so hard on (for eleven minutes) and quite possibly ruined her life. I retreat to my computer. Minutes later she walks by clutching a sixty-nine-cent thrift-shop bowl in her hand. Headed to the back door, she says, "I'm going to go break this against a tree."

One of my favorite childhood memories was the Day of the Bowls. I had told Jack and Margaret about it several times. One afternoon, John, Liz, and I were bickering so much that my mother had had enough. She went to the kitchen and came back with three bowls. Honest-to-goodness china cereal bowls from our cupboard. She calmly handed one to each of us and said, "Don't come back inside until you've broken your bowl."

We looked at her as if we had finally succeeded in driving her insane. She'd been on the brink before when we would not stop fighting in the car or when dinner and homework and arguing and a drafty old house became too much.

I didn't want to break my bowl. It just seemed so…bad. Liz couldn't wait to take out her aggression on hers, and I gave no mind to what my big brother thought—perhaps that he was trapped in a household full of crazy women.

Out we traipsed to break our bowls. Our driveway was gravel, so no amount of dropping did the trick. We hurled them against trees. I have no idea what we'd been fighting about, but we were soon over it, laughing at how very strong our stupid bowls were, and wondering if Mom would ever let us back in the house. Had she locked the doors? The Day of the Bowls lives on in our minds as creative parenting and a bonding experience.

And now decades later, fed up with me, with life, and with no brother to fight with, Margaret, chin jutted out, is ready to break a bowl. I look up at her, careful not to smile or frown. I remain neutral, glance at her bare feet and say, "Make sure you put some shoes on."

I have writing to help me get out my feelings. Tim has running and his Bible study groups. Margaret needs an outlet too. I'm proud of her for knowing she's angry and finding a way to deal with it. For opening that cabinet door and getting out a bowl. And a cheap one too. She may not yet be able to put voice to her feelings, but instead of yelling at me right now, she's finding a constructive way to express them.

She comes back in five minutes later, her face red from crying.

Damn bowl wouldn't break.

forty-six

I pull up to my friend's river cottage for three days away by myself. The farther away I get from the highway and from the congestion, the easier my breathing becomes and the more relaxed I feel. I've been feeling burdened lately just having to live and try to make decisions for our family.

The idea behind my time away is to help me get a handle on my writing and to give Tim and Margaret a break from me. I'm nervous about being on a river. I don't know what to expect, and I've had some trauma being near water since Jack's accident. Our family used to love to be outdoors and did a lot of hiking near creeks, but if *this* river looks anything like a creek, I don't know if I can handle it.

After stepping into the cottage, I see the view out the big back windows. Beautiful, calm water for as far as I can see. A sloping green lawn reaches down to a tiny sandy beach, maybe eight feet wide, and the Potomac River laps soundlessly onto the sand. There are no woods, no rapids, no sheer drop-offs here. It looks more like the ocean, and I am not afraid.

I take my shoes off and head out into the grass, where I am greeted by a small yellow lab. When I look up, I see a man, just a few years older than me, sitting on a metal glider, enjoying a cigar. I pet the dog and then walk over to meet the man, who lives in town but comes to his cottage on "the rivah" each evening to relax.

If this were a horror movie, I'd tell him I'm staying here alone to write a book, and then he'd come back a few hours later, a maniacal Jack Nicholson smile on his face, to do me in.

If this were a Nicholas Sparks novel, the dog, smelling Shadow on me, would keep coming over from his lawn to mine, until the man invited me over for a beer and then, well, you know. We'd find out his wife left him and I was recently widowed (sorry, Tim!) and the healing power of the river and the bald eagle family soaring overhead would bring us together.

But this is neither a horror movie nor a novel, so I go inside and watch TV, wondering if I'm good enough and strong enough to write a book. I wonder if breaking into my friend's unopened box of Thin Mints is poor form. I wonder if the words *Sharing Size* on my bag of M&M'S represent a command or just a suggestion. I fall asleep on the couch.

I write on and off the next day and the next, and I fantasize about our family having a small place like this to spend quiet Christmases or go crabbing in the summer. I realize I am only picturing three of us, not Jack too. Would it work, or would it be too quiet for Margaret? Would we always have to invite a friend? I don't know.

I don't know how any of this will work, our future with a fictional riverside cottage or not, but in this brief moment, in this place, it doesn't feel too horrible to consider.

forty-seven

I don't know when I begin to feel better. Maybe it's when a "mom-sized" serving of ice cream—the scoop after scoop bowlful I used to dish out to the kids to try to fatten them up—starts to taste good again. Maybe it's a dinner out with friends that I don't have to force myself to go to, and where small talk doesn't make me want to scream curse words. Or maybe it's looking forward to a new season of our favorite TV shows, when just months before, everything we watched or did seemed intolerable and off-putting, and any plans we made were just another meaningless way to occupy a few hours. But I do begin to feel better. Glimpses of light and lightness begin to permeate my days. I guess I would say I begin to feel less stricken.

I can go to the grocery store and think about apples. I still think about Jack and his final snack of apple slices with peanut butter as I count out apples and put them in my bag, but the memory passes into and then out of my mind without paralyzing me. I can take a walk around town without feeling exposed and vulnerable. I can begin to think about making plans without feeling like I'm betraying Jack.

One day I carry cans of spray paint upstairs from the basement. Margaret, on her kitchen stool, sees me and her eyes light up. "Are you painting something? Did you finally get your mojo back?" I'm surprised by how excited she is to see a glimpse of the old me, even though I'm really just cleaning out the basement.

She wants me to care about what I used to care about, to have at least one thing go back to the way it was before. The new me who pours out her heart on the Internet and shares tea and tears with other moms who have lost kids does not impress her. I think she wonders if every new person I meet has lost a child. Margaret wants me to pick up furniture from the side of the road again, to fret aloud about whether I should sand a piece first or just paint it. I tell her

I'm not painting anything and her face falls, but I notice inside me the feeling that it wouldn't be too far-fetched if I ever got out my drop cloths again.

I wonder if all of this is just my getting used to having Jack gone, the way you eventually get used to losing a limb, and the way we adjusted to our subpar shower situation before finally getting it fixed. Or could it be acceptance? I'm not sure. But I begin to feel better. I feel more hopeful, not just for heaven someday, but for life today. I'm not doing anything differently than a few months ago—going to work, taking care of Margaret, writing, getting to-gether with friends—but it all starts to feel a little less horrifying.

Just a few months ago, I was riding with Jenn on the highway when she almost hit a car in the next lane over. For a few seconds it seemed like I was going to end up sitting in the driver's seat of the other car. Jenn apologized profusely for almost killing us, and I said, "Please. Do you really think I'd care at this point?" I don't know what has changed in the months since, but I don't want to die anymore, at least not yet.

forty-eight

Tim and I climb into the car and pull out of the carport. Margaret is already at the campground a few hours away with my sister's family. This trip starts so differently from those in the past: silence, no kids in the car, just two adults wondering why we are even bothering.

On those other trips, I'd pray out loud as we sat in our driveway. "Please God keep our family safe and bless our time together." We'd pull onto our street, and right after we'd round the first corner, Tim would pat the top of his head, then his chest pocket, and we'd turn around to get his glasses that sat on the tray next to the TV remotes. The kids and I would laugh. The rhythm of those trips was predictable. Now, few things are.

I think of the mother of the murdered girl in the book *The Lovely Bones* who cut and ran. She ditched her family and went out west to work in a vineyard. I did not respect her decision, although I could see why she'd made it. It feels tempting as Tim and I begin our drive. But I'm more of a stayer, a sifter, a sorter, than someone who runs away. Usually.

We could have bagged our annual camping trip, but we really, really want to try it. Tension that hung between us as we packed, which was really just anxiety about trying to make this trip, diffuses and is gone by the time we hit the curvy mountain roads and pull up to our usual camping spot. A handful of suntanned teenage boys, including Jack's favorite cousin, Isaac, toss a ball around and grab cheese balls by the handful out of a huge plastic barrel. Jack loved that damn barrel of cheese balls.

Margaret and the rest of the crew are about to go tubing on the river. I haven't seen her in almost a week as she's been visiting my sister, so I say I'll go too, even though I'm nervous. I want to reconnect and be brave.

Margaret and her cousin pull out ahead of me with the teenagers and adults, guided down river by the gentle current. So much for catching up. Before I know it I'm sharing a raft with three chatty elementary-age kids we've known for years but only see on these trips.

Once we start down the river, there will be no getting out for the next two hours; we must float where the river takes us. No cutting and running here. Our first camping trip without Jack, at our same familiar campsite, floating on a river of...WATER...and being charged with keeping three kids alive. It is a lot.

In some ways it couldn't be better. I have to stay focused on the children, so I'm less focused on missing Jack and all of our camping memories. Also, little kids have no filters, so our conversation ranges from the joys of peeing in a river to "I'm just so sorry Jack died." "We miss Jack." "Now, what exactly happened to Jack?" "Does a body keep growing once it's buried in the ground?"

I explain that Jack's body was cremated, which means it was burned up, not buried. "I'd hate to have to watch that," says one of my little buddies, and I agree that I would too. We talk a little about God and a lot about their classmates at school and spiders. It feels good to just get it all out there. How many times have I wanted to say to someone, "I'm just so sorry So-and-So died" but have held back because I'm not sure if it's an appropriate time?

On the raft, I must be the responsible adult, the cheerleader, the motivator, not just the broken one, and it feels right. A huge bald eagle swoops down and sails right over us then on up the river. We whoop and cheer. Nature is beautiful. Yes, it is dangerous and unpredictable, but it is also good.

At one point our raft gets hung up on a tree stump in the water. This has never happened to me before. I can't dislodge it for some time, and I become afraid. This wide, peaceful river is nothing like the raging creek that took Jack's life. Nothing. But I'm still frightened.

It starts to rain. Great. We decide that we are cold, tired, scared, hungry, and we all have to pee. During our time stuck, as the water rushes around me and I stand on slippery rocks trying to dislodge the raft, I tell the kids that this would be a great time for us all to pee, so we do, and we laugh, our teeth chattering and our lips turning blue.

A few minutes later, we are safely ashore again, ready for campfires, fried food, and millions of twinkling lightning bugs. Just a few months earlier, this trip would have been an impossibility. Now it is difficult, but doable.

This summer we have found ourselves trying to make decisions about our family's future. It has been a mix of discerning when to revisit the traditions of the past and when to cut and run. We see that there is not one right way.

And I am glad we chose to camp.

forty-nine

We carry box after box of Legos to my friend's car, trying not to break apart the buildings, creatures, and vehicles that Jack built. It's raining, of course, because why shouldn't it be when I'm packing up my dead son's things so we can put the house on the market? It is miserable, holy work.

I love our house. It's nothing fancy, but the memories here are tender and precious to me. I'm pretty surprised to be in this situation, even after everything that's happened. I like to bloom where I'm planted, living in my hometown, teaching in my old high school before our kids were born, and even working right down the road in the church where I grew up. After Mom died I spent ten years among her things until my father sold the house.

There was great comfort in wandering the rooms, touching what her hands touched, kissing her photographs, rubbing my face against her clothes in the closet. I took my time when it came to the sorting and donating, and that felt right to me.

I'm sure many people assumed, immediately after Jack's accident, that we would move. How could we stand living on this street? Passing the house where it happened? Driving over the creek every single day? Seeing all the neighborhood kids playing? Trying to forge a new life when Jack's room stands empty down the hall?

They probably couldn't picture our staying, but I couldn't imagine leaving. Moving seemed like the worst possible option, making our lives all the more cruel and unfair. Jack was the ultimate homebody, and the idea of leaving his place, our place, sickened me.

Sure, we can take his things with us wherever we go, but when his treasures are moved, no longer placed by his careful hands, will they cease to hold meaning? I can revisit conversations and memories in each room of this house. I can hear his voice. To leave would be one more loss, and have we not hit our limit?

So for almost two years, we stay. I'm comforted sitting on Jack's stool at the breakfast counter. Spreading out on his twin bed, trying to remember what it felt like to have my arm wrapped around his middle, his hand resting on my arm, my face in his hair. Leafing through the books he was reading. Letting myself feel the pain as his Yankees wall calendar stays on September 2011. Admiring his building projects that stand unfinished and interrupted, like his story. Smelling his clothes, once again, and praying that his scent would somehow linger.

When we leave this house, we'll leave behind the thread that dangles from our bedroom doorknob where we tried to pull out one of Margaret's loose teeth. It didn't work, but I still remember her squeals and Jack's laughter. We will leave the growth charts marked on two-by-fours, and their handprints in green paint on the wall in the unfinished basement. We will leave the screened porch where we did math drills and read books, and the pantry where Jack and Margaret squeezed together on the top shelf to "surprise" me as I walked into the kitchen, their giggles giving them away.

I guess we'll have to throw away his toothpaste, his toothbrush, and the uneaten Crunch bars a classmate's mother gave him on the first day of school. And what will we do with his retainer? Now these things can sit precisely where he left them, but is packing it all up and moving it someplace else just ridiculous? I don't want to have to make these decisions.

I am terrified that if we leave this house, we will somehow leave Jack behind. I do not want to run away from my memories of this home, this love, because the beautiful ones far outweigh the painful ones. Also, I wonder if moving could be "the Thing" that finally breaks us.

But I know I am not blooming here anymore. When the kids were small, I asked Jack what my superpower would be if I had one. He answered, "Going to the bathroom all the time!" He knew my bladder well. But I consider my two greatest gifts, which don't come from any strength of my own or anything special I've done, to be good mental health and the ability to be real and open with people.

Staying here jeopardizes both of those. I think of the image Jack showed Courtney shortly after the accident, of me standing looking out a window, not being comfortable inside or outside the house. How accurate that has been! Jack showed her he was helping me, and I believe he has been, but staying here has become almost unbearable. But so is the idea of leaving. I thought if I just toughed it out through the first year it would be become easier to live on the street where the accident happened. But it hasn't. I find myself growing anxious and hopeless, and I wonder if I can continue to take the pain and stay sane. I can feel it wearing on Tim and Margaret too, even though their struggle isn't as overt as mine.

So Tim and I make the painful decision. We will move. Leaving our home is one more loss, and it makes me angry and sick. But I come to truly believe it will be best for the three of us. Margaret is completely opposed. She has never known another home. Her memories of Jack are linked to every tree, every handprint, every room.

After making the initial decision to move, I must begin to sort through more than ten years of family life. One day, Margaret walks into Jack's room as I'm on the floor, sorting through his school papers and projects. I'm grateful he was a saver, because there are many glimpses of him here. I can't believe some of the creative sentences he came up with to liven up boring grammar assignments. If I'd seen them at the time, I would have been annoyed, but now it's like hearing from Jack anew.

I like the way he used all the correct parts of speech to vilify the writers of his grammar workbook and the pointless, repetitive assignments they doled out. Margaret leans over, and I read a few of the funny sentences to her. I wonder if she can hear his voice in her head as I read. She smiles, then says, "That makes me miss him even more."

Me too.

I hand her a Target gift card I've found among his things, one of many Jack had saved up from birthdays or Christmas. "Here. This is for you. Let's go shopping." I reach out my hand, and she helps pull me up. We head out and within an hour she has picked out a navy-blue polka-dot dress and an expensive bottle of nail polish.

It's not a small thing for her to spend Jack's gift card this way, on something so very Margaret and entirely un-Jack. It has taken many months to get to this point. Margaret has been on alert, protecting his room and his possessions. Have I moved things around? Did I disturb the Lego minifigures on his dresser? Have I thrown anything away? For a few weeks I set up a folding table and my computer in his room, hoping to get inspiration for my writing. She didn't like having my papers spread all over his bed.

I think back to what Courtney told me, that Jack says Margaret "has dibs" on his room, that it does not need to be a shrine. He must have known how important, almost sacred, his room would seem to her, with all his treasures lined up carefully on the shelves, each Lego scene laid out in a precise tableau. Jack was giving her permission to let go.

We haven't rushed it, but Margaret is starting to see that what's his is hers and that she can't make any wrong decisions about any of it. Jack, so careful with his room, his money, and his possessions, doesn't need them anymore. So we go shopping, and he buys her a new dress.

Although Tim says he wants to move, he drags his feet. Months pass. He is too busy to make small repairs. He is fearful about selling our house before we have somewhere else to go, but we can't afford to buy a new one first. That uncertainty is hard on him, and I'm tempted to give up. To decide to wait until we have more time, more money, and more energy for this task. But because I'm hopeful that moving will help all of us, I push ahead with the purging, the fixing, and the packing, drawing on a strength I'm not sure I have.

So on this rainy Thursday, Margaret's last day of school before summer, I finish packing up Jack's room so she won't have to see me do it. She'll check with me later to make sure I've taken pictures of every shelf, every vignette that Jack had planned and placed just so. Thank goodness I have.

I hand box after box of Legos to Jack's friend Cortland, who will watch over them until our house sells and we find another place to live. I try not to let Cortland see me crying, but my red nose and eyes give me away. He asks if he can have Jack's basketball hoop, and I say, "Sure, we don't need it anymore." His mom seems embarrassed by his asking me, but I love it. I want him to have something of Jack's.

I can't believe how tall Cortland has gotten; he seems more like a man than the boy Jack knew. I look down at his iridescent green sneakers and gasp. His feet are enormous. What a contrast to Jack's small black suede sneakers that sit by the door of this room. I bought them before school started, but he never got a chance to wear them.

They are the last thing I pack.

fifty

I was really looking forward to Jack becoming a teenager. I taught high school for years before the kids were born, and Jack already reminded me of the adorably awkward boys who would stand at my desk, intent on telling me weird facts before class started. They cracked geeky jokes that went over the heads of the more popular kids, but that always got a little chuckle from me.

When Jack was in sixth grade, he found out it was his science teacher's birthday. They had been talking about all different kinds of rocks in class, so when he came in from recess, he proudly presented her with a rock he'd found outside, calling the specimen a "Common Rock." She took it home and put it on her fireplace mantel. I'm doubtful Jack would have become the full-fledged geek that I hoped for, but a mother can dream.

When he was eleven, I already had a sense of our little-boy time being short. And even though I looked forward to his teenage years, I anticipated missing the times he would want to snuggle and would confide everything to me. It was time for summer camp, so he and I made the four-hour drive to Pennsylvania, listening to an audio book on the way. We stopped at Taco Bell for lunch and a little while later pulled into the camp parking lot.

Something was wrong. Where were the counselors with their weird hats and alarmingly large smiles? Where were the other cars? Jack and I got out of the car and looked around. The camp was completely empty. My face fell. "Oh no!" I said. "I think camp starts tomorrow!"

Rather than blaming me for my screwup, Jack just smiled and waited to see what we were going to do. I called home to tell Tim that we'd be spending the night in Pennsylvania. There was no way Jack and I were going to drive another four hours home, just to do it all again tomorrow. Instead, we walked around the little town. We went into antique shops. "This is good training for you for when you get married," I said, and he gave me that familiar embarrassed smile.

We went to the tiny toy store, and he sat and played with puzzles and logic games while I watched. It was a wonderful feeling not to rush him, and as he leaned his head over the puzzles, I could remember him as a little boy and the many agenda-less days we spent together before life got busy and we got distracted. We wandered into a drugstore and bought snacks and a toothbrush. Then we headed to a motel in a nearby town.

Just as we were about to get out of the car, a torrential rainstorm started. We waited it out, listening to the audio book, then spent the rest of the afternoon under the covers of our comfy beds, watching the World Cup on TV. That night we went out for a nice dinner together. The next day we slept in, something we could never do when sharing hotel rooms with our early birds, Margaret and Tim.

Camp didn't start until late afternoon, so we drove to see Frank Lloyd Wright's Fallingwater, nestled deep in the woods. Jack had always wanted to see it, because being an architect was on his short list of careers. I didn't spring for tickets to see the inside of the house, so he and I walked along the paths and stood on the terraces, listening in on other people's guided tours and taking pictures.

Even at the time, I knew our unplanned getaway was significant. Instead of beating myself up about my mistake or worrying that I was stuck wearing the same underwear two days in a row, I was able to just enjoy my time with Jack. I called it our "bonus time." In the gift shop we bought Margaret a book. I was tempted to buy Jack the Lego set of Fallingwater, which I knew he would love, but I didn't.

There is regret that I didn't buy him the Legos and didn't spring for the more expensive tickets, but most of all there is gratitude. I am grateful for the gift of that time with him, and I can bring it up in my memory when the burden of the accident, the falling water that took him from us, feels so intense.

I can say to him, "I love you, Jack, and I loved my time with you." I miss him, and I always will, until we are together in a place much better than this one, built by the greatest Architect of all.

epilogue

Full Hearts

Our new house sits just a few miles down the road. In a hot real-estate market, we found only one house for sale in our price range and jumped on it. We were determined to get Margaret settled before middle school started, and we scraped in with just a few days to spare. The floor plan is almost exactly like the old one, which has been more comforting than disconcerting.

The round table fits right under the window in the kitchen. My office is in the same place too, so I've written this book in a setting almost identical to the one where I blogged all those years. We haven't figured out where to put Jack's Legos yet, so they are stacked in row after row of copy-paper boxes, awaiting our next step. His clothes are in his dresser in the guest room. I'm not ready yet, but maybe someday we'll make them into a quilt to keep us warm while we watch TV.

I was terrified that in leaving the old house I'd lose even more of Jack, but it doesn't seem that way at all. There is a feeling of lightness and relief in my days. I guess when you are forced to let go of what is most precious to you, it's a little easier to let go of other things, like a house. Or my cell phone, which broke on moving day. I didn't want to replace that old phone because of the comfort it brought us on the night Jack died and several key times since, but it wasn't the phone that was so special anyway; it was the message that nothing could separate us from God's love, not even raging water, death, or grief. Friends who have visited our new home say they feel Jack's presence here. Our new house provides a balm we were looking for.

From my new kitchen window, I see children playing in the street, but since they never knew Jack, it doesn't feel as if he should be out there with them. Putting time and space between Jack's neighborhood buddies and me has helped soften my heart in a way I just couldn't manage earlier.

Tim can easily reach his running trails from here, staying active in the way Courtney showed Jack encouraging him to do, and it's not unusual for him to log more than a dozen miles before Margaret and I wake up on a Saturday. In addition to coping through exercise, he continues to foster deeper relationships with his friends. He has stepped up every time I've needed extra support with Margaret and has grown more flexible as we navigate the unknown.

We continue to grieve Jack's sweet soul in our own unique ways, both together and separately. Most mornings Tim will start the *Washington Post* crossword puzzle, then leave it on the table for me to finish up. If I start it first, I'll leave a few sections for him, mainly the ones about sports and science. We're pretty good at coming up with what the other needs and when, like the way we take turns lifting each other up on the hard days. That our marriage has survived, and will continue to survive such devastation, feels to me like something of a miracle, and I don't take it for granted. Each day is a new opportunity to show each other grace.

Margaret is successfully navigating the world of middle school at a large public school. Although she misses the family atmosphere of her small elementary school, she has met tons of new people who get to know her for her fun personality, big smile, and quick mind, not just her family's story. And even though she wouldn't let me throw away any of Jack's things when we moved, she feels comfortable in our new home with much of his belongings still packed away.

As Margaret ages past Jack, I believe he will remain her older brother, looking out for her and cheering her on as he always did. He is not as far away as he may seem. My prayer for Margaret is that as she grows older, she'll remember that the same God who gave her the uncanny knowledge that Jack would die, and who sent angels to get her away from the creek, is always with her, and that she can do great things with the strength He gives her. As her special Bible verse says, "You are mine."

———

Shortly after Jack died, I met with Paula, the wife of one of the paramedics who had tried to save Jack. She told me that my example of courage and faith is inspiring people. "Why do people think I have such a strong faith? My faith feels so tiny!" I asked.

"It just flows out of you, Anna," she said.

I realize that there is little I can or cannot do about what flows out of me, whether it is raw grief, faith, or inexplicable hope.

Ask me on a Wednesday and I'll say that Jack's death is part of God's beautiful plan for the world and that every action and every second of that terrible Thursday had to happen in order for that plan to be fulfilled, though my human eyes are too clouded to see what it is. Ask me on Friday and I'll say we live in a sinful world where bad things happen to good people and while an all-knowing God let this happen to Jack—even gave us a foreboding of what was to come—He didn't make it happen. Other days I won't say anything at all. I mean, what do I know?

I'm certainly not willing to drag other hurting mothers into my brain games as I try one idea or another on for size. I'm not going to tell a mother whose first grader was gunned down in a classroom that it was part of God's plan. I may be there with Jack's death on more days than I'm not, but I refuse to come to these conclusions for anyone else.

And it's tricky. Because hurting people want to understand; we want to know why. But we don't want people coming to conclusions *for* us, feeding us neat little answers of what God's will is and how His mind and heart work. No thank you.

I guess the only thing that is certain to me now is that the small God I followed before, the one I must secretly have believed would spare my family pain if I just didn't ask for too much or set my sights too high, is somehow not big enough to carry me now.

That little God isn't the one who comforts me when I despair. No, it's a big God, whose loving voice reminds me of my mother's, who gently whispers to me, "I know, Anna. I know, honey. I know."

I understand now there is no way to get an A in grief. I can just be honest about my feelings, try to live gently with others, and when that's too hard, give myself a little break and find some distance. I can commit to plucking out the seeds of bitterness about how unfair life is when they sprout up again and again as they have on these pages. I can decide each day to trust that God knows what He's doing.

I've learned to be open to the mysterious ways God chooses to reveal Himself, even when doing so makes me feel a little like the weird dad I judged so harshly in the very first grief book I read.

Mostly, what I'm still learning is yet another way to look at Jack's favorite Bible verse, "For nothing is impossible with God." Jack used that verse to encourage himself in doing hard things, despite life's challenges. Then, with the accident, the verse seemed to mock me. For (even with) God, nothing is impossible! Our precious child could die! Eventually, it revealed itself in a third way: God can give comfort through birds, rainbows, dreams, visions, clouds, and signs. Why had I thought that a holy God wouldn't or couldn't use those means to show His love? *Nothing* is impossible with God. And finally, I've been learning that with God so close to me in my heartache, what I thought was impossible is possible, surviving and perhaps eventually thriving despite losing my Jack.

While cleaning our office before the move, I find a note Tim wrote for Jack when Jack was two and a half. Tim planned to give it to him when he was older.

October 2001

Jack,

Every night we would read books to you and say your prayers before you went to bed. Twice this month after we said your prayers, you put your hands on my face and said, "I'm filling your heart with life." I'm not sure where you learned that, or if you made it up, but it was very touching. You do, indeed, fill my heart with life.

Love, Dad

Even in death, Jack continues to fill our hearts with life. I can feel it. It's the love between a parent and a child that can't be snuffed out or drowned or stolen. It's hope for heaven—not a boring eternal rest, but a vibrant, purposeful existence with God that continues to affect what is going on right here, right now.

Even two years after the accident, I continue to experience surprises. Hard ones, like the ambushes of grief when I'm just going along and the full weight of our loss overtakes me. How it hurts so much to hear the sound of a high school marching band wafting through the trees and realize Jack will never go to a high school football game or a homecoming dance.

And beautiful surprises like the two blue jays that sometimes swoop down to our feeder, to join the flock of titmice and cardinals and downy woodpeckers that seem to have followed us from our old house. Or the tiny little brown bird that flew into our kitchen last week, hung out on the windowsill awhile, then flew back out again.

discussion questions

1. After her son dies, Anna affirms, "Jack was well prayed for. . . . Prayers of courage. Prayers of protection." She asks, "Was it all a crock?" Ultimately she concludes, "We can't keep our children safe. . . . We don't know what the future holds." What is your response to this? Are you shocked by the author's bluntness? Is it a truth you've already discovered? How? If you are a person of faith, how does this idea affect your beliefs?

2. When Anna realizes that Jack has been carried away by the creek, she writes, "I don't know how I know at that second that Jack will die, but I do." Have you ever experienced a "knowing" prior to a disastrous event? If so, what was that intuition like, and what did you do about it? On balance, is "knowing" a good thing or bad? Why?

3. Anna mentions the verse Jeremiah 29:11, "Which we . . . had used as some sort of blanket promise that life would be okay, sure seems like a load of bullshit to me now." Discuss a time the scriptures that once comforted you suddenly felt like salt in a wound. As time passed, did you remain alienated from the Bible and/or God, or did you change over time?

4. In the hours after Jack's death, Anna receives what she regards as two signs of God's kindness: a silhouette made by flashlight of Jack's profile and a Bible passage that popped up on her phone. Have you ever experienced God showing up in unexpected and apparently coincidental ways and times?

5. "Standing in this little cemetery on this gorgeous September day, I feel like I've been forced onto a scary, dangerous amusement-park ride, constructed by a psychopath, not a loving God." Does Anna's visual

strike you as apt and true? Can you relate to the idea of being forced into a terrifying situation against your will?

6. For months, when Anna goes to school to pick up her daughter, Jack's classmates come to hug her. "I try not to act greedy or needy. I am starved for a touch from Jack's people, his tribe. . . . They tell me Jack stories, . . . offering them to me as precious jewels." When you were in the midst of enduring calamity, was there something you craved but didn't recognize until someone supplied it?

7. While some friends avoid her, a few seek out Anna to talk and cry with her. "I'm grateful that they, clueless and scared, will venture into the grief with me." Anna confesses that she herself has been "a drive-by friend. . . . I'm the type of friend you would want around for a broken ankle but not for chronic depression." Are you the type who avoids others' grief or one who walks right into it? Why?

8. As the author struggles to make sense of Jack's death, she finds, "I can't believe in a God who would take my son in order to make me more compassionate, loving, or holy. I'm afraid that would be a deal breaker." What issues are nonnegotiables in your relationship with God?

9. Anna finds that she and her husband grieve differently. She wants to "cocoon" at home and spend quiet time together as a family. Tim wants activity, hobbies, even to do things he once did only with Jack. How do you and your partner face grief or tragic circumstances? How are you alike—what keeps your bond strong even as you cope in unique ways?

10. Before and after the accident, people see visions and have dreams of Jack. Anna is encouraged yet also concerned that these apparitions are self-created. What do you think about such signs and wonders—are they wishful thinking or something more?

11. *Jack is dead. I will not kill myself today. Help us!* This is Anna's daily prayer as she slogs through the adjustment to her loss. When you've experienced loss, did you pray? Was it helpful? Were there things you could not bring yourself to say?

12. Anna begins talking to Jack, saying small things like "I love you, Jack" and "I'm sorry, buddy." She acknowledges, "It feels good to speak into the silence . . . to say the words in present tense. Because my love is not in the past." Do you speak (aloud or silently) to people you've lost? Why or why not?

13. As the one-year anniversary of Jack's death arrives, Anna and Tim find themselves grateful for friends who've stayed close. "They let themselves get muddy and wet . . . [from] tears and the messiness of grief, both ours and their own. These relationships and the friends . . . who have supported us are in some ways the collateral gains of our losing Jack." While it may seem inappropriate, even offensive, to think of "gains" in relation to loss—have you found any in your seasons of grief?

14. One day Anna realizes she is better: she feels less vulnerable in public; she enjoys the taste of ice cream; she makes plans; she can buy apples without focusing on their being Jack's last snack. "I don't know what has changed in the months since, but I don't want to die anymore, at least not yet." When have you turned a corner in your recovery from something? Was there a catalyst or did pain just finally ease up, even microscopically? What would you say to someone who is sure things will never get better?

15. "I'm packing up my dead son's things so we can put the house on the market. It is miserable, holy work." What activity have you found awful but necessary, even valuable? What events or rituals have you experienced as holy? Does the sacredness of something terrible soften the pain of it?

16. Have you found, as Anna did, that "in times of heartbreak, God is closer than our own skin"? Why or why not? If so, how? How does this affect the way you are approaching your future today?

acknowledgments

Thank you to Stacy Morrison and Rebecca Gradinger for helping me see, even when the wounds were still so raw, that this story could become a book. Thank you, Heather Kopp, for being the best memoir doula around. Your guidance and prayers helped move me forward, and our friendship is one of the sweetest fruits of this experience. Thank you, David Kopp, for the gentle way you encouraged me, called me a writer, and provided the support I needed. Heather and David, there is no way this book would have happened without you! And thank you to Nicci Jordan-Hubert for helping me face the tricky stuff head-on. Thank you to Stephanie Dolgoff for helping me trust my instincts and for talking me down when I felt stuck. Thank you, Glennon Doyle Melton, for encouraging me to just be myself.

Dear friends Cindy Parker, Emmy Parker, and Mariann Alicea, thank you for offering up safe refuges in which to write, cry, and watch bad TV, and mostly for letting a brown-eyed boy touch your hearts.

A huge thank-you to the blogging community and *An Inch of Gray* readers who showed up for me every single day, despite the painful subject matter. You gave me a reason to keep on writing. You taught me that true friendships and community often take place in the middle of the night and through a computer screen. I want you to know that your support played an important role not just in the writing of this book but in my survival. Thank you for sharing your lives and stories with me. For those I've been able to meet and hug in person, it has been my honor. I look forward to meeting the rest of you!

Thank you to my "rocks"—the old and new friends who have walked beside me—whether for forty years or for three. Cynthia, Meredith, Cindy, Jenn, Dawn, Jena, and many others who have each played a special role in my healing. You know who you are.

To Tim, Margaret, and Liz, thank you for everything. I don't always understand this life, but I'm so grateful to be doing it with you. We have passed through the waters together, yet they have not swept over us. We have walked through the fire, yet we have not been consumed. If what doesn't kill us makes us stronger, we must be beasts by now! I love you!

And to Jack, who made me feel like the best mom in the world, even if I was at my worst. Thank you for being my son. I love you. I miss you. And I'll never forget you.

about the author

A graduate of James Madison University and Wake Forest University, Anna Whiston-Donaldson taught high school English before becoming an at-home mom and writer. Her part-time work in a church bookstore solidified something Anna already suspected—books can change lives. Anna began blogging at *An Inch of Gray* in 2008 and has been featured twice as one of BlogHer's Voices of the Year. When her family lost twelve-year-old Jack in 2011, Anna was buoyed by the love and support of the online community. Anna enjoys thrift shopping and finding curbside treasures, and she will gladly take you on a "dumpster dive" tour of her house. Speaking to groups and encouraging women to connect with each other are two of Anna's passions. Anna lives outside of Washington, DC, with her husband, Tim; daughter, Margaret; and chocolate Lab, Shadow. To learn more about Anna, please visit annawhistondonaldson.com.

Printed in the United States
by Baker & Taylor Publisher Services